Statesmanship

Statesmanship

Six Modern Illustrations
of a Modified Ancient Ideal

Wendell John Coats, Jr.

SUP

Selinsgrove: Susquehanna University Press
London: Associated University Presses

Associated University Presses
440 Forsgate Drive
Cranbury, NJ 08512

Associated University Presses
25 Sicilian Avenue
London WC1A 2QH, England

Associated University Presses
P.O. Box 338, Port Credit
Mississauga, Ontario
Canada L5G 4L8

The paper used in this publication meets the requirements of the American National Standard for Permanence of Paper for Printed Library Materials Z39.48-1984.

Library of Congress Cataloging-in-Publication Data

Coats, Wendell John.
    Statesmanship : six modern illustrations of a modified ancient ideal / Wendell John Coats, Jr.
        p.   cm.
    Includes bibliographical references and index.
    ISBN 0-945636-84-9 (alk. paper)
    1. Political science—History.   2. Liberalism—History.
3. Statesmen—Cast studies.   I. Title.
JA81.C58   1995
324.2′092′2—dc20   95-14824
                                                                          CIP

For Pamela, who still believes. . . .

Contents

Preface

THIS BOOK GREW OUT OF A SENIOR SEMINAR I HAVE TAUGHT AT Connecticut College since 1987. My explicit interest in the idea and practice of statesmanship evolved during the years from 1981 to 1984, while I was visiting professor of political science at Kenyon College, and for one year a visiting fellow at the Public Affairs Conference center there. A version of the first chapter was presented as a paper to a panel of the Society for the Study of Greek Political Thought in Chicago at the 1992 annual meeting of the American Political Science Association. So far as I am aware, my approach to analyzing statesmanship in the modern world is beholden to no one in particular; thus, I alone am responsible both for its insights and its errors. Thanks to Leslie Rubin, Pamela Jensen, and Dirk Held for reading and commenting on parts of the manuscript; and to Dawne Roberge and Tina Falck for their assistance with typing.

Introduction

IN THIS BOOK I ATTEMPT TO ASCERTAIN HOW MUCH OF THE ANCIENT
Greco-Roman ideal of statesmanship and oratory can be carried
into modernity without logical contradiction and irrelevance.
Thus the book's central question is a theoretical one, but (in the
hope of greater clarity than typifies the scholastic debate on the
relevance/irrelevance of "antiquity" to "modernity") the answers
are sought through inspection of, and reflection on, actual historical instances of statesmanship. I believe this is an important
question for our time, because of forces and developments that
threaten to efface the conditions making the arts of statesmanship
and politics—properly understood—possible and viable. (If we
are going to put aside even our more truncated modern version
of statesmanship, it is of at least some value to be clear about what
we will be giving up and what it has made possible for us.)

The central challenges to the pagan ideal of statesmanship are
collected in the first chapter and include Christianity in its various
evolutions; modern liberalism in the context of large, modern,
comparmentalized, and differentiated states and economies;
and the effects of modern science and technology and their in-
stitutionalization in our daily lives.[1] An initial account is then
attempted of those features of statesmanship which can accommodate themselves to the outlook of the liberalism of the past three
centuries (without logical contradiction and without loss of practical meaning).

There follows a series of chapters on the careers of some modern leaders beginning with Washington and ending with Nixon
and Kissinger. These cases were selected on the basis of their

capacity to test and supplement the list of statesmanlike characteristics enumerated in the first chapter. Often the outlook of "practitioners" is considerably different from that of contemporary
political theorists and sheds light on what are considered important problems in the academic discipline. For example Washington's explicitly Ciceronian orientation is interesting in this
context, by coherently combining an emphasis on property and
commerce with devotion to public service for the common good,
something some modern theorists say is contradictory.[2] And
Churchill's defense of the power of oratory explicitly addresses
and deflects the modern argument about its irrelevance to politics
in large, modern states. The chapters on Wilson and Lincoln are
especially (though not exclusively) concerned with illustrating the
dangers for statesmanship in millennialism or the attempt to alter
the fundamental structure of political reality through the use of
traditional political means. The chapter on de Gaulle (like the
one on Churchill) is especially useful in illustrating the explicit
application of ancient views to modern politics, and the chapter
on Nixon and Kissinger addresses some new dangers for the practice of statesmanship.

The final chapter rehearses the characteristics of statesmanship
that were seen to be compatible with the outlook of modern liberalism. Said differently it attempts a formulation of statesmanship
in the terms of modern, nonteleological language. It then attempts—against the views of both mild and strong millennialism—a statement of those conditions which must abide if the
arts of statesmanship and politics are to endure as the *primary*
basis for cooperative efforts among human beings in proximity.

This book is intended for two separate audiences and hopefully
has something to say to each. Students and (potential) practitioners of politics and statesmanship, who simply intuit that
these arts still exist and believe that the point is to practice them,
will hopefully find interesting the substantive judgments made in
the chapters on various statesmen. Another hope is that they
would take away (in at least the backs of their minds) an appreciation of potential contemporary dangers to the continued practice
of these arts and the general conditions that nourish them. But
the book is intended to address as well aspects of the debate within
the discipline of political theory over the relevance for modern
politics of ancient Greek (and Roman) political thought. In my
view the most interesting implication of this study in that context

is that the insights of the ancient city-state theorists are applicable with the least qualification (to the political life of large modern states) at the highest levels of leadership, during the gravest of crises, and for the highest stakes, that is, during historic moments of such intensity[3] that the inescapable necessity of comprehensive and decisive political leadership for the continued viability of a civilized way of life simply presents itself.[4]

Statesmanship

1

From Ancient Writers toward a Theory of Modern Statesmanship

THE ARGUMENT OF THIS BOOK IS PREDICATED ON THE ASSUMPTION that the ancient Greek (Aristotelian) idea of the art of political rule has relevance to the study and practice of politics in the (relatively) modern world, because a commonsense appreciation of something equivalent to it has been present in the understanding of important political leaders and practitioners such as Washington, Churchill, and others (up until at least the very recent past). The aim here is to present an account of the characteristics of the arts of statesmanship, beginning with reflections of Plato, Aristotle, and Cicero, and the assumptions or postulates necessary to make this art intelligible in a theoretical discussion directed toward distinguishing it from similar and related forms of leadership and rule.

Working from the thoughts of Plato and Aristotle on political rule and Cicero on oratory, I propose to fill in an initial sketch of statesmanship, which, in turn, will be modified to accommodate the reduction of the scope of politics and political rule introduced by Christianity and the subsequent secularization of many of its ideas, including those congenial to the rise of modern science and modern liberalism. Let us begin with some of the ideas in Plato's dialogue, *The Statesman.*

PLATO, "THE STATESMAN" (POLITIKOS)

When this dialogue between "young Socrates" and the "Stranger" finally returns to the express subject of its title, here are the ideas about statesmanship, or the art of rule, that emerge. First is the distinctively Platonic idea that statesmanship is a form

17

of knowledge, more exactly a craft *(techne)*, which molds citizens following the divine model of justice by imitating or approximating it in the realm of political life.[1] Based on other Platonic dialogues such as *The Republic,* we know that this idea of justice requires a certain ordering of the individual *psyche* (and the political regime) such that the intellect rules other qualities and those individuals imbued with greater intelligence rule those with less. Now I believe it is not necessary to accept this particular complex of Platonic ideas to be able to avail ourselves of the other ideas about the art of statesman in this dialogue. That is, the others do not logically demand this one, which can be replaced by some idea of the common good or common advantage, politically ascertained, with violating the coherence of what follows. Let the reader judge.

The other major complex of ideas about the art of rule in *The Statesman* has to do with distinguishing it from related arts, in particular, generalship or strategy, the art of public speaking or persuasion, and the art of administering legal justice.[2] As it turns out the real art of rule is the architectonic art or the art that controls the work of these and other arts, deciding when to develop and use them:

> *Stranger:* If you will view the three arts. . . . You will be bound to see that none of them has turned out to be the art of statesmanship. This is because it is not the province of the real kingly art to act for itself but rather to control the work of the arts which instruct us in the methods of action. The kingly art controls them according to its power to perceive the right occasion for undertaking . . . the . . . enterprises of state. . . . It is concerned with laws and with all that belongs to the life of the community. It weaves all into a unified fabric. . . . It is a universal art.[3]

The analogy of weaving a unified fabric is then extended to include the idea of blending the influence of two distinct and recurring types of citizens—the moderate and the spirited or vigorous—because the extended ascendancy of either spells the decay of the body politic:

> *Stranger:* Men who are notable for moderation are always ready to support peace and tranquility. . . . Because of their indulgence of this passion for peace at the wrong times, whenever they are able to carry their policy into effect they become unwarlike themselves without being aware of it and render the young men unwarlike as well. Thus they are at the mercy of the chance aggressor. . . . What then is the history of the party whose bent is rather toward strong action? Do we not find them forever dragging their cities into

war and bringing them up against powerful foes. . . . Either they destroy their country altogether, or else they bring it into subjection . . . just as surely as the peace party did. . . . The statesman sets about his task of combining and weaving together these two groups exhibiting their mutually opposed characters.[4]

Now, in the account of Plato's Stranger, this weaving analogy is extended to include techniques even for inducing the proper genetic unions (i.e., the intermarriage of the vigorous and the moderate). Although we may not care to follow his prescriptions this far, it certainly is possible to accept the idea of statesmanship as a general or comprehensive art that attempts to combine coherently the competing claims of various arts (strategy, oratory, judging) and various types of citizens in the interest of the good of all, through the use of various techniques, as well as the important ability to instill a conviction of unity in all:

> *Stranger:* Do we realize that it is the true statesman . . . who alone is able . . . to forge by the wondrous inspiration of this kingly art this bond of true conviction uniting the hearts of the . . . folk of whom we were speaking just now.[5]

Holding these ideas in mind, let us now turn to Aristotle's thoughts on political rule to see what modifications and additions he makes to Plato's account.

ARISTOTLE'S POLITICS

Like Plato's Stranger, Aristotle begins his discussion of the scope of statesmanship or political rule by identifying it as the universal or architectonic art, concerned to direct other arts such as economics and strategy and all types of citizens.[6] But he qualifies the art of political rule more than the writings of Plato by drawing out what is implied in the word "political." Political rule in its truest sense, for Aristotle, is distinguished from the mastery of monarchs, parents, and slave owners, because it is exercised over those who are free and equal, for the good of those who are ruled, and by those who have been, and will again be, ruled by others:

> the good citizen must possess knowledge and the capacity requisite for ruling as well as for being ruled, and the excellence of a citizen may be defined as consisting in a knowledge of rule over free men from both points of view.[7]

... there is ... rule of the sort which is exercised over persons who
are similar ... to the ruler, and are similarly free. Rule of this sort is
what we call political rule; and this is the sort of rule which ... the
ruler must begin to learn by being ruled and by obeying.[8]

The good political ruler or statesman, in Aristotle's view, is one
who employs that blend of prudence (moral wisdom), persuasion,
and coercion called politics to direct fellow citizens toward the
goals of the particular regime or constitution involved, excluding,
it would seem, monarchy, tyranny, and extreme democracy—re-
gimes all characterized by situations where the political art is,
carefully speaking, either superfluous or impossible. Statesmanship for Aristotle, then, may be seen as equivalent to the art of
instituting and sustaining practices and habits of political rule
between rulers and citizens.

CICERO

We have seen that Plato's Stranger and Aristotle both view oratory or the art of persuasion as the subordinate part of the statesman's art, but it is interesting to compare this point of view with
that of the first century B.C. Roman republican, Cicero (who knew
Greek and had read Plato especially). Cicero, who had no single
word for statesman (or politics), tends to treat the art of persuasion as something akin to statesmanship itself in one of his dialogues. Perhaps in reaction to the view of the mature Socrates (in
Plato's *Gorgias*) that rhetoric or the art of persuasion was no art
at all but rather a form of flattery or deception. Cicero has a
sympathetic character make a similar but grander claim for the
art of persuasion in his dialogue, *On the Orator.* In this dialogue
the character Crassus asserts (like Socrates of *The Gorgias*) that
there is no separate art of speaking but rather only real knowledge of the various arts and professions addressed. Crassus says
of the ideal orator that he must know human nature, he must be
learned in the liberal arts, and he also must

know all about our law and our statutes, he must have a thorough
understanding of ancient history; he must master the usages of the
Senate, the nature of the constitution, the rights of the subject allies,
our national treaties and agreements, the interests of our empire. And
finally he must be able to sprinkle a little salt on his speech.[9]

Cicero's Crassus would appear to claim for the art of oratory what "The Stranger" claimed for the art of statesmanship in Plato's *Statesman*, that is, the comprehensiveness of a universal art. But elsewhere, in the essay *On Duties*, writing his own name, Cicero treats the art of oratory or public speaking in a more commonsensical, Aristotelian way, as a subordinate art, useful in conducting affairs and building support:

> For what is better than eloquence to awaken the admiration of one's hearers or the hopes of the distressed or the gratitude of those whom it has protected. . . . The door of opportunity . . . is wide open to the orator whose heart is in his work.[10]

Nor when Cicero writes in his own name does he make such comprehensive claims (as does his character, Crassus) for the knowledge or the orator, implying perhaps by his silences on the question that it is sufficient if the orator *knows something about* the arts and professions he addresses and attempts to direct.

Summary of the Ancient View

Drawing upon some of these reflections from the ancient world on the requirements for good political leadership, let us attempt an initial statement of the art of statesmanship, which does not seem immediately alien to our modern views. As I see it we are discussing an art or profession directed toward attending to the major affairs of a body politic of formal equals in the interest of the general or common good, which employs "politic" or moderate means whenever possible (before resorting to even legal coercion), such as deliberation, persuasion, and compromise and which requires the abilities to inspire convictions of unity and form character in citizens. This art also requires some understanding of the various types of human beings in any community or city or state, as well as the various professions or crafts that sustain it and make up its life—financial, military, legal, pedagogic, and so on. This art or activity, then, is distinguished by its aim (achieving the general good in meeting a stream of contingencies), its scope (the major activities in the life of a people), and its means (political, i.e., a blend of persuasion and coercion within the framework of fundamental laws, reflecting prudent judgment).

Before turning to the consideration of historic instances of this activity in subsequent chapters, let us consider, by way of further refinement of our definition, several salient objections which might be, and have been, raised to the theory and practice of this practical ideal.

STATESMANSHIP AND CHRISTIANITY

One major conflict with the aims and methods of this pagan ideal appeared in the teaching of Jesus Christ and its influence as subsequently institutionalized in the Christian religion (especially its Western European versions). As is well known, Christ preached a revolutionary way of relating to others that inverted the natural hierarchy in which the intelligent and strong dominated the less intelligent and weak and asserted the superiority of the meek and childlike to the wise and prideful. This teaching, in fact, rejected more than the order of pagan nature, disdaining as well the ancient Hebraic law of "an eye for an eye," and providing only a single maxim for dealing with political authority: "Render unto Caesar the things that are Caesar's, and unto God the things that are God's."[11] In combination with the dual allegiance to the Pope and Caesar, which arose in the Western church, the salient effect of Christ's teaching on the pagan view of politics and statesmanship was its virtual suppression, at least for several centuries. St. Augustine's well-known account of the duties of citizens in Book XIX of *The City of God* (fifth century, A.D.) simply admonishes them to follow St. Paul and obey earthly rulers as long as they demand nothing contrary to faith, because their very function is to provide for earthly peace and concord between believers and nonbelievers and between the peaceful and the violent even among nonbelievers:

> So, too, the earthly city, that lives not by faith, seeks an earthly peace. . . . Whereas the heavenly city, or rather the part of it that goes its pilgrim way in this mortal life . . . needs must make use of this peace too. . . . Therefore, so long as it leads its life in captivity . . . being a stranger in the earthly city . . . it does not hesitate to obey the laws of the earthly city whereby matters that minister to the support of mortal life are administered to the end that . . . a harmony may be preserved between both cities with regard to the things that belong to it.[12]

And, on the same point, Augustine says:

> While this heavenly city ... goes its way as a stranger on earth, it
> summons citizens from all peoples, and gathers an alien society of all
> languages, caring naught what difference may be in manners, laws,
> and institutions by which earthly peace is gained or maintained ...
> provided that there is no hindrance to the religion that teaches the
> obligation to worship the one most and true God.[13]

This Augustinian solution of "limited government" to the dualism of realms introduced by Christianity would appear to have
more in common with modern liberal pluralism (and such a link
can be established by way of Augustine's influence on the makers
of the Protestant Reformation a millennium later[14]) than with the
theory and practice of the later Holy Roman Empire. I cite it here
for its clear recognition of the distinction *between* the realms of
nature (and politics) and grace. The Thomistic "synthesis" some
eight hundred years later (after the reintroduction of Aristotle's
Politics and *Ethics* into Western European intellectual life), with its
view that grace perfects rather than destroys nature, is recognizable as more typically Roman Catholic.[15] Yet the evolution of the
Thomistic solution to the dualism of realms also illustrates the
urgency of the problem which arises when political order is
treated as outside of the realm of grace but the entire civilization
has become nominally Christian.

Asking the reader to bear in mind that my point here is to show
that the ideal of statesmanship has survived in an uneasy tension
with the outlook of Christian civilization and its subsequent liberal
mutations,[16] I turn to the writings of Niccolo Machiavelli (especially *The Prince*) as an illustration of what can occur when the
tension becomes too uneasy. And I try to dramatize my point by
showing how the pagan Cicero can give advice similar to that of
Machiavelli yet in the name of rectitude rather than ruthlessness.

In several dramatic chapters in *The Prince*, Machiavelli plays
upon the gap between the individualist orientation of Christ's
teaching ("resist not evil," "turn the other cheek," "judge not")
and the requirements of political leadership concerned with and
responsible for the fate of many individuals. Consider in this light
several infamous injunctions from *The Prince*. First Machiavelli
accepts the Christian or individualistic definition of virtue over
the pagan or political usage:

> The fact is that a man who wants to act virtuously in every way neces-
> sarily comes to grief among so many who are not virtuous. Therefore,
> if a prince wants to maintain his rule, he must learn how not to be
> virtuous, and to make use of this or not according to need.[17]

He then goes on to give illustrations of being "unvirtuous" that
play for a dramatic effect on the paradox that possible ethical
choices for individuals as such make less sense for the person in
charge of the practical, earthly fortunes of many. For example
Machiavelli observes that a prince, in order to gain a reputation
for generosity, should not give away the resources of his own state.
This will only force him to take more from his subjects to keep
things afloat, which will, in turn, gain him the reputation of a
miser. A prince is more likely to gain a reputation for generosity,
paradoxically, by being parsimonious.[18]

On the issue of obtaining a reputation for compassion, Machiavelli notes that this is more likely gained through severe rather
than lenient action toward law-breakers; the latter course may
lead to major civil disorders over time, which will only result in a
reputation for cruelty toward the community as a whole: "It is far
better to be feared than loved if you cannot be both."[19] On the
issue of honoring one's word, Machiavelli observes that in the case
of a prince, who speaks not only for himself but his state, this is
not always possible if the state is to survive against others who
deceive and employ treachery. And, here as well, we may note that
Machiavelli accepts (in contrast to Plato's Socrates, for instance,
who devised a "golden lie" for the good of the city of *The Republic*)
that usage in which deception for any purpose is evil: "As I said
above, he should not deviate from what is good, if that is possible,
but he should know how to do evil, if that is necessary."[20]

Consider, now, in the context of "individualist versus political
ethics," several illustrations from Book III of (the pagan) Cicero's
famous essay on duties *(De Officiis)*. In this work Cicero adopts
the Platonic theme that what is right and what is expedient are
never at odds, and he attempts to illustrate the maxim for a Roman audience (including his own son to whom the essay is addressed). But, as we shall see, what is right for Cicero is not
defined in the context of an individual conscience standing directly before an omniscient (personal) God.

Is it morally right, asks Cicero, to kill a tyrant? Not only is it
right, he answers, but even noble. "Has expediency, then, prevailed

over moral rectitude *(honestum)?* Not at all: moral rectitude has gone hand in hand with expediency."[21] Furthermore, because we have no ties of fellowship to the tyrant, "it is not opposed to Nature to rob, if one can, a man whom it is morally right to kill."[22] Is it morally right for a wise man to "take the bread of some perfectly useless member of society?" In this case it depends on the motive: the answer is "yes" if the intent by remaining alive is "to render signal service to the state and to human society."[23] Is it morally right to break one's promises, asks Cicero? Again, it depends: if the issue is life, health, or the good of one's country, then, "yes,"[24] and so on.

The general point here for our analysis is that in the name of moral rectitude Cicero can give advice that sounds "Machiavellian" to us because he has not inherited the dichotomy between the realms of nature and grace or between imperatives for the health of the community and an individual conscience before an all-knowing and all-caring God—a gap that all of Western statecraft, since Constantine, has had to bridge, whether through some sort of theoretical synthesis, duplicity, silence, or at least "short shift" as in the case of Winston Churchill:

> The Sermon on the Mount is the last word in Christian ethics. . . . Still it is not on these terms that Ministers assume their responsibilities of guiding States . . . the safety of the State, the lives and freedom of their fellow-countrymen . . . make it right and imperative in the last resort . . . the use of force should not be excluded.[25]

> It is baffling to reflect that what men call honour does not always correspond to Christian ethics.[26]

Indeed one of the very few pieces of analysis ever to admit this tension head-on, and attempt to deal with it, is to be found in a public lecture by the German sociologist of religion, Max Weber, on the differences between an acosmic "ethics of ultimate ends" and an "ethics of responsibility." Delivered in 1919 the lecture makes the following claims:

> He who seeks the salvation of the soul, of his own and of others, should not seek it along the avenue of politics. . . . The genius or demon of politics lives in an inner tension with the God of love, as well as with the Christian God as expressed in the church. This tension can at any time lead to an irreconcilable conflict. Men knew this even in times of church rule.[27]

Weber (who, incidentally, suffered two nervous breakdowns) then goes on to suggest that perhaps these two ethics are not "absolute contrasts" but can be united at the moment when the "mature man," with a "calling for politics," follows the ethics of responsibility as far as it permits, and only then invokes an acosmic ethic of ultimate ends with Luther's words: "Here I stand; I can do no other."[28]

STATESMANSHIP AS CRAFT OR TECHNE

There is another difficulty that suggests itself in applying a pagan idea to the modern world of liberal democratic politics, but again we shall find that it has already been worked out at one level by those who created the modern world. This is the Platonic idea that the rule of the statesman is a *craft (techne)* which molds "citizen-matter" into preexisting "forms." Modern sensibilities rebel at the thought of such a curtailment of individual self-expression by rulers, just as medieval thinkers rejected the pagan idea that earthly rulers and philosophers could know the final form or end for any human soul. But this problem has already been worked out in its political version by thinkers such as Hobbes and Rousseau in the modern idea of sovereignty or the "sovereign will":

> The government is not the supreme authority in the modern state as the ruler is in the Platonic Polis, but is subordinate to something of which Plato did not possess the conception: a sovereign will. The presence of sovereign will in a state makes only relative the subordination of subject to rulers. . . . The governor himself is only a minister of the sovereign.[29]

> The organs of the sovereign will in a democratic State are . . . Free Speech, Press, Party, Universal Suffrage, and Representation. . . . They are not the means by which the ruler exercises power upon the subject, but the means by which the sovereign exercises power upon the ruler.[30]

Obviously if constitutions become so "democratic" in practice that virtually every act of the ruler is subject to immediate (or, even preemptive) control through popular referenda, then there is little for even our modern, attenuated version of statesmanship.

But where such a situation has not yet arrived (and no government can last for long once it does arrive), there would seem room for a circumscribed craft of statesmanship or political rule if two conditions are present. First the sovereign and the ruler must still have some idea or conception of what political rule is and why it is desirable, and second, they must have some power to give effect to this complex of ideas, especially in the face of resistance to it from whatever quarter and for whatever reasons. And, although this will become clearer throughout these studies, an essential element in the idea of political rule is the activity of *politics* (and the deliberation and moderation that accompany it) as the basis for reconciliation of differences within the body politic.

STATESMANSHIP AND MODERN ECONOMICS AND TECHNOLOGY

In an oft-quoted passage from *The Wealth of Nations* (1776), Adam Smith, one of the fathers of modern economics, warns statesmen about meddling with the laws of supply and demand:

> I have never known much good done by those who affected to trade for the public good . . . every individual . . . can in his local situation, judge much better than any statesman of lawgiver can do for him. The statesman, who should attempt to direct private peoples in what manner they ought to employ their capitals, would . . . assume an authority . . . which would no-where be so dangerous as in the hands of a man who had folly and presumption enough to fancy himself fit to exercise it.[31]

This passage does not mean that Smith rejected all political controls over economic matters—he supported the "navigation acts" during times of danger, for example; nor does it mean that there is not room for debate over the degree to which economic matters can and should be regulated, depending on a society's other priorities, the industry concerned, and the needs of the moment. (Do we really believe that the "free market" and all its effects are right for everyone, everywhere, and at all times?[32]) The point in Smith's discussion for our theme about the applicability of the ancient idea of statesmanship to more modern times is simply that the purview of statesmanship is again circumscribed—but it is not excluded from some oversight of the activity concerned. Aristotle's observation that the political art must know something, but not everything, about economics and finance seems relevant still. Even in liberal democracies that leave much latitude for the dynamic of supply and demand in production and allocation of goods and services, there are still important political decisions affecting and controlling the fate of economic activity, for example, defense and other public sector-spending decisions, tax laws, monetary regulations, and so on. Furthermore even governmental decisions restricting government's own interference in economic matters are *political* acts.

The situation is similar with the development of complex technology. Although, like the interplay of supply and demand in the market, technology has impulses toward its own autonomy, there has been agreement across the political spectrum (from marxism to liberalism) of the need for *some* political or human control over its directions, for example, over weapons research, use of nuclear energy, residual environmental effects, DNA research and experimentation, use of computers for record keeping on citizens, and so on. The general point is that, like the modern cultivation of the creative and spontaneous in the realm of the spiritual and political, modern economic and technological "imperatives" circumscribe, but do not eliminate, the possibility for the art of statesmanship or political rule. In fact it may turn out to be the case, as computers come closer to approximating the capacity for human judgment (e.g., the ability to make sense of random events), that the practice of statesmanship affords the best chance for the preservation of a public space for human spontaneity.

Statesmanship and Political Technique

Because statesmanship describes a practical activity, the appellation, "statesman" or "stateswoman" must, it would seem be reserved for instances of rule and leadership that reflect both "good intentions" and some "success in results." The good intentions can be assumed in patterns of conduct, indicating a concern for the welfare or the common good. Success in results usually is evidence of some combination of skill and luck[33] on the part of the statesman.

The skills in question, in my view, break down into roughly three areas. *First* is the distinctly statesmanlike skill, following the ancient Greek view of politics as the master or architectonic art, of judging when to employ and develop the other "arts" (e.g., diplomatic, financial, military, and so on). A part of this skill, in turn, is simply the capacity to see and function consistently (especially during periods of either boredom or crisis) at the proper level of abstraction or generality. But another part of this general skill is dependent on a *second* area of skills, that is, some substantive knowledge of the "subordinate" activities and professions involved—legal, commercial, military, parliamentarian, etc. (Is this not why we still prefer national leaders in the highest offices to have had a range of professional and other experiences?) A *third* distinct area of skills contributing to success in the art of statesmanship concerns those expressly useful in building alliances or bases of support, for example, ability at public and private persuasion, diplomacy, endurance, and a working knowledge of the *types* of human beings afoot, including what is likely to be persuasive and motivating for each type, under varying circumstances, from normal to extreme.

These latter skills involve the kinds of techniques usually described in "political handbooks" (for example, "keep your enemies in front of you," it's not who you know, it's who you get to know," "don't get mad, don't get even, get ahead"[34]) though they rarely can be expertly acquired simply from books. The general point for our analysis is that though statesmanship is not constituted exclusively in such skills and techniques for staying afloat in the sea of politics, it cannot be present without them either. Often political leaders who appear to have no interest in such techniques (such as Lincoln, for example) have had such mastery so as to employ them without making them obvious.

What Statesmanship Is Not

If, as was suggested above, statesmanship can be stipulated and identified in terms of *aims, scope, and means,* is it absolutely necessary that a candidate for statesmanship "measure up" in all three areas? Without being pedantic or legalistic, I believe this must be the general case if statesmanship or political rule is to distinguish itself from other forms of rule, such as mastery, domination, and "management."

The relationship between statesman (or stateswoman) and citizen is clearly different from that between military commanders and subordinates, between priest and parishioners, between administrators and administered, and between scientist and roleplayers in an experiment, for example, because none of these rely in any essential way on political *means* of persuasion and alliance building. And the relationship between statesman and citizen differs from that between managers of economic or corporate enterprises and their employees, in the reduction of scope and generality of purpose, that is, in the failure of the common corporate enterprise to rise to a sufficiently general and complex level as to require a political vocabulary to describe it. But what about instances where the leadership in question is more ostensibly "political" or concerned with public forms of comprehensive authority? As a general approach, it is necessary to scrutinize carefully the activities in question from the standpoint of the aims, scope, and means of statesmanship, as we have laid them out thus far. For the sake of further illustration, let us consider two specific cases that require more careful analysis than might at first be supposed—the American politician, governor, and senator, Huey Long, and the founder of the (now defunct) modern Soviet state, Lenin.

THE CASE OF HUEY LONG

The dying words in 1935 of U.S. senator and former governor of Louisiana, Huey P. Long, were reported to be, "God don't let me die. I have so much to do."[35] What did Long still have to do, and what had he already done? Huey Long had presidential aspirations in 1936 as a step to the White House by 1940. He thought that if he could dilute Franklin D. Roosevelt's support in 1936 by splitting the democratic vote with a candidate of his own choosing, allowing four years of a republican administration, the country would be ripe for his radical nationalization program ("Share Our Wealth") in 1940, sentiment for which had already driven Roosevelt farther to the left by June 1935 than he ever intended.[36]

And what had Long accomplished in his own state during his tenure as governor? He had done much for the great mass of poor and dispossessed, at the expense of the powerful (especially large corporations): "the great road and bridge program, the improved free hospital services, the free textbooks and increased appropriations to schools, the free night school for adults, the

debt moratorium and homestead exemption laws, and the aboli-
tion of the poll tax," to name the most obvious. And there were
other accomplishments that benefited all. Long had built up the
state university, introduced "rational" administration into Louisiana's midlevel civil service, and preserved the state banking system
(only seven Louisiana banks failed) during a depression.[37] Furthermore Long clearly possessed know-how in the means of politics—oratory, coalition-building, parliamentary, legal, electoral
tactics, and so on. Yet, in spite of the scope of his vision and
his mastery of political techniques, Huey Long's accomplishments
(and unaccomplished goals) cannot be viewed as "statesmanlike"
on our model. Neither his aims nor some of his methods qualify.

Long's aims (which no doubt became more perverse as his
power in Louisiana grew more complete) were not to establish
practices of moderate, political reconciliation among relatively
free and equal citizens but rather to consolidate his own power
by keeping the largely unpolitical masses content (and unpolitical)
by providing them with a better living standard.[38]

> He rejected . . . the charge that he was a dictator. . . . But . . . he was
> frank enough to admit that his control over his own state was abnor-
> mal in an American commonwealth. But Louisiana was still a democ-
> racy, he insisted. "A perfect democracy can come close to looking like
> a dictatorship, a democracy in which the people are so satisfied they
> have no complaint," he once suggested.[39]

It is clear that Long was not interested in developing the civic
responsibility of his fellow citizens as part of his leadership, much
less in preserving even a modicum of independence in his political
competitors (though he never pursued former rivals into private
life once they were driven from power). His methods and political
machine virtually eliminated normal parliamentary practice; bills
were sometimes passed in minutes with no one present but
Long,[40] and eventually became ends themselves:

> He wanted to do good, but to accomplish that he had to have power.
> So he took power and then to do more good seized still more power,
> and finally the means and the end became so entwined in his mind
> that he could not tell whether he wanted power as a method or for
> its own sake. He gave increasing attention to building his power struc-
> ture, and as he built it, he did strange, ruthless, and cynical things.[41]

For our purposes, it is not necessary to ascertain Huey Long's ultimate aims and motives if they could with any certainty be ascertained, or if he himself knew. It is enough to show that he was *not* interested in eventually establishing and maintaining a situation similar to what, following Aristotle, we have called political rule over fellow citizens.

THE CASE OF LENIN

Statues of the maker of the modern Soviet state have been taken down throughout the former Soviet Union. Yet, only several years ago, one could find American students prepared to write papers defending Lenin as a statesman for industrializing Russia and other countries and "bringing them into the twentieth century" (at whatever human expense)—and this in spite of Lenin's explicit rejection of the traditional vocabulary of statesmanship and politics as "exploitative."

The case of Lenin is useful for our purposes, because in addition to being a practical revolutionary, he made his general views explicit and put them in writing, retaining enough of the intellectual baggage of Marx and Engels to allow illustration of why an outlook directed to permanent (for at least the foreseeable future) revolution is inimical to statesmanship, political rule, and moderate politics. Several years before his death, Lenin distilled his mature views on the technique of revolution and put them in a manual ("'Left-Wing' Communism—An Infantile Disorder"), which has been called "his political masterpiece."[42]

Lenin's "manual" is interesting for its blending of the visionary promises of Marx and Engels about the elimination of life's major "contradictions," *with* a most detailed account of the techniques necessary to foment and sustain the world revolution putatively ending in such a visionary condition. Here is Lenin's own definition, which makes clear his rejection of the activity of moderate politics on principle:

> The art of politics . . . consists in correctly gauging the conditions and the moment when the vanguard of the proletariat can successfully assume power.[43]

And, on Lenin's view, the old politics was counterfeit anyway, serving only to disguise a class conflict that needs to be made explicit in the interest of its own elimination.

The dictatorship of the proletariat means a persistent struggle—bloody and bloodless, violent and peaceful, military and economic, educational and administrative—against the forces and traditions of the old society. . . . Without a party of iron . . . such a struggle cannot be waged successfully.[44]

To prepare the conditions for the rise to power of the "vanguard of the proletariat" means using a number of old political techniques, including those of "bourgeois parliamentarism" but all merely as steps for the effacement of the old politics and the ushering in of a new era which will:

eliminate the division of labor among people . . . educate and school people, give them all-round development and an all-round training, so that they are able to do anything. Communism is advancing . . . towards this goal, and will reach it.[45]

For purposes of our analysis, it is sufficient to note that Lenin's (and Marx's, for that matter) starting and ending points are a principled rejection of politics and statesmanship as the (moderate) solution to the reconciliation of differences among people. I also note here, in passing, another aspect of all variants of marxism, which, if accepted, makes statesmanship unlikely if not impossible. This is its extreme elevation of the status of practical human activity (*praxis*), a point explicitly made by the twentieth-century, French intellectual, Maurice Merleau-Ponty in his book, *Humanism and Terror:*

Marxism rested on the profound idea that human perspectives, however relative, are absolute because there is nothing else and no destiny. We grasp the absolute through our total *praxis* . . . or, rather men's mutual *praxis* is the absolute.[46]

Such a romantic outlook, if accepted, blurs the conditional status of practical activities such as politics and statesmanship, making them both grander than they can be and smaller than they should be, and calls to mind Aristotle's observation that if man were the highest being in the cosmos, then politics would be the highest activity.[47]

SUMMARY

I have attempted to show that a modern idea of statesmanship can be formulated, which draws upon the ideas of, especially, Aristotle; and I shall try to show in the chapters that follow that it can be and has been applied to the public life of the modern liberal world over the past two centuries (by its practitioners if not by its theorists). In its purest sense it equates to the idea of political rule, where· "political" is understood to mean a comprehensive or "architectonic" perspective focused on molding character and leading fellow citizens through a stream of contingencies, within the context of fundamental laws (a constitution), and through primary reliance on a mix of persuasion and coercion called "politics."[48] We have seen the directness of this activity's control diluted over two millennia to accommodate demand for greater individual spiritual, moral, legal and economic autonomy, and creativity, but, as I have tried to suggest here and will try to illustrate in the various case studies that follow, not yet diluted to the point where the idea of statesmanship fails to make a meaningful and useful distinction.

Said differently we still need the word or concept to describe a particular kind of rule and leadership, observed perhaps more often in the breach than in practice but still important both as a theoretical idea to account for events and as a practical ideal to be *kept in mind* by the actual practitioners of politics as they go about their business. And, if economic and technological planning "imperatives" are destined to efface this particular form of "societal integration" in the future because, in especially its modern, liberal version, it afforded too great a latitude for individual human judgment to permit efficient "resource management,"[49] then analytic exercises such as this one are perhaps justified on the rather dismal grounds of maintaining clarity about what we are about to forego.

2

George Washington and Alexander Hamilton

I TREAT THESE TWO AMERICAN FOUNDERS TOGETHER BECAUSE HAMilton never held the nations's highest office and because some of his ideas about directions for the United States found direct effect under Washington's administrations. I also treat these two together to illustrate why, in spite of the similarity of some of their views, Washington is the more "statesmanlike" figure and the one with the sounder and more comprehensive outlook. (John Adams's notorious quip that Hamilton had made Washington his "tool"[1] seems to me way wide of the mark, a misperception perhaps engendered by the very breadth and distance of Washington's perspective.) But, above all, I treat these two together because both were military men (Hamilton was an artillery officer and later Washington's aide-de-camp during the Revolutionary War) as well as founders, and the *decisiveness* requisite for both activities permits illustration of the differences between two functions of statesmanship, that is, one concerned with getting constitutional arrangements in place, and the other with employing them to deal with the daily stream of contingencies facing a body politic.

It is this latter function of statesmanship that demands more of the expressly political skills of persuasion and alliance building, activities in which Washington and Hamilton were neither especially adept nor interested, though Hamilton attempted to imitate some of Jefferson's techniques of local organization near the end of his career.[2] And, in fairness to Jefferson, if he was more interested in the business of what we would now call "politics," he was also capable of thinking and functioning as a founder when the issue became one important for *his* more democratic vision for the new country. (For example, Jefferson was prepared, to act decisively and in an ambiguous constitutional capacity to acquire the *material* basis for a vast new empire from a desperate Napoleon Bonaparte.) We shall return to the differences in orientation *between* Washington-Hamilton *and* Jefferson later on, as a way of illustrating the hierarchic relationship between these two functions of statesmanship, that is, the dependence of the daily kind on the founding kind, an important insight with practical consequences which grows more obscure as a founding recedes in time.

Let us now take up the career of George Washington from the standpoint of the light it may shed on the general characteristics of statesmanship. First there is the capacity for a comprehensive or "universal" outlook. In my view Washington's greatest strength as a statesman-founder was his recognized ability to bring together in coherent vision the various activities involved in the "business of a nation" and *sustain* this focus without wavering, allowing others to marshall their energies within and behind it. In the comprehensiveness and coherence of his vision, in my view Washington was superior to even Hamilton. Let me illustrate.

Washington's letters, addresses, and actions over his political life-time reveal a coherent vision of connections among ostensibly diverse activities, a vision more characteristic of classical or Renaissance culture than that of the modern world. (Even Washington's contemporaries were cognizant of Washington's lucid capacity for "linking things together."[3]) We find in Washington's outlook an attempt to link together in the life and leadership of the new nation ideals that the modern world would channel into categories such as pedagogic, civic, moral, religious, military, economic, legal, and political. In fact a vision such as Washington's extended into so many ostensibly disparate fields that it could probably only have had practical effect at the time of a founding or beginning, even in the eighteenth century. In brief Washington's vision was for bringing together habits of (ancient) civic and military discipline, modern religious sensibilities, and modern personal and property rights and freedoms, in institutions that would perpetuate and harmonize them. Consider, in this context, several of Washington's writings, at different periods, starting with the "circular letter" to the states in 1783, at the close of the Revolutionary War, setting forth a vision and account of the work that lay before them all. (Even as a military commander, Washington was always thinking of the political union which must follow.)

Washington begins the letter by stating his intention to retire from service of his country but wishes as his "last official communication" to offer his "sentiments on some important subjects." I shall try to summarize Washington's views thematically here, because my aim is to show the *breadth* of subjects addressed as part of a *coherent* vision. Washington begins by calling before the minds of his readers the auspiciousness of the historical moment:

> The citizens of America . . . are, from this period, to be considered as the Actors on a most conspicuous Theatre, which seems to be particularly designated by Providence for the display of human greatness and felicity. . . . Heaven has crowned all its other blessings, by giving a fairer opportunity for political happiness, than any other Nation has even been favored with.[4]

In addition to its natural resources and the freedom deriving from its recent military victory, the new nation has been born at a "happy conjuncture of times and circumstances." Washington then goes on to *link* up the birth of the new nation with the state of civilization generally:

> The foundation of our empire was . . . laid . . . at an Epoch when the rights of mankind were better understood and more clearly defined, than at any former period; the researches of the human mind, after social happiness, have been carried to a great extent. . . . the free cultivation of Letters, the unbounded extension of Commerce, the progressive refinement of Manners . . . and above all, the pure and benign light of Revelation, have had a meliorating influence on mankind. . . . At this auspicious period, the United States came into existence as a Nation.[5]

Washington then asserts that "this is the moment to establish or ruin the national character forever," that is, to consolidate the federal government to realize its promise or to relax it sufficiently to "become the sport of European politics." His analysis of the present crisis and opportunity goes on to link together liberty and sovereign authority, showing how the former depends on the latter:

> Liberty is the Basis. . . . Whatever measures have a tendency to dissolve the Union, or to contribute to violate or lessen the Sovereign Authority, ought to be considered as hostile to Liberty and Independency of America.[6]

In this "circular" Washington also highlights the importance of paying the debts that Congress had a right to incur in order to

prosecute the war, including the back pay for regular officers of
the Continental Army:

> In this state of absolute freedom and perfect security, who will grudge
> to yield a very little of his property to support the common interest
> of Society, and insure the protection of Government.[7]

Washington then urges the creation of a regular militia to con-
stitute a "proper Peace Establishment" for "the defence of the
Republic," reminds all of the deficiencies which they recently ex-
perienced firsthand owing to "the want of adequate authority in
the Supreme Power," and concludes with a prayer of admonition
that the citizens of the United States will "cultivate a spirit of

> obedience to Government, (and) . . . a brotherly affection and love for
> one another . . . which were the Characteristiks of the Divine Author
> of our . . . Religion, and without an humble imitation of whose exam-
> ple in these things, we can never hope to be a happy Nation.[8]

In other addresses and letters, we see the same themes picked
up, elaborated upon, and held together in coherent perspective.
First there is the link between politics and the transcendent. In
Washington's writing one sees the recurring conviction that the
"finger of Providence" is at work in the events of the incipient
founding of the new nation. This is always mentioned with a sense
of wonder. Here is a typical paragraph on the subject, in this case
in a private letter to Lafayette in May 1788:

> A few short weeks will determine the political fate of America . . . and
> probably produce no small influence . . . through a long sucession of
> ages to come. *Should every thing proceed with harmony . . . it will be so
> much beyond anything we had a right to imagine or expect eighteen months
> ago, that it will demonstrate as visibly the finger of Providence, as any possible
> event* in the course of human affairs *can ever designate it.* It is impracti-
> cable for . . . anyone who has not been on the spot to realize the
> change in men's minds . . . which will then have been made.[9]

And on the same point, in a more public capacity, here is Washington in his first inaugural address, April 1789:

> No people can be bound to acknowledge . . . the invisible hand which
> conducts the affairs of men, more than the people of the United

States. *Every step which they have advanced . . . seems to have been distinguished by some token of providential agency.*[10]

Washington's first inaugural address also makes clear that his concern for the "transpolitical" extended to the subpolitical (for the modern world) realm of private morality as well: "The foundations of our national policy will be laid in the pure and immutable principles of private morality." This idea is developed at greater length in the farewell address, in a paragraph that shows Washington's own (rather than Hamilton's or Madison's) sentiments:

Of all the dispositions and habits which lead to political prosperity, Religion and morality are indispensable supports. In vain would that man claim the tribute of Patriotism, who should labor to subvert these. . . . Where is the security for property, for reputation, for life, if the sense of religious obligation *desert* the oaths . . . in Courts of Justice? . . . *reason and experience both forbid that National morality can prevail in exclusion of religious principle.*[11]

In between that cosmic responsibility for the future of republican government and liberty and the moral habits of individual citizens of the United States, Washington, of course, saw need for the institutional devices of the Constitution, combining reciprocal checks on power, with a national executive capable of vigor and decisiveness, when necessary. Still among the most influential of the founders, it is Washington who places the greatest emphasis for the future of free government on the character of individual citizens and leaders.[12] Hence his emphasis on education for elites, including the proposals for a military academy and a national university, was to teach principles of republican government:

Amongst the motives to such an institution, the assimilation of the principles, opinions, and manners, of our countrymen, by the common education of a portion of our youth from every quarter . . . in the science of *government*. In a republic, what species of knowledge can be equally important? and what duty more pressing on its legislature, than to patronize a plan for communicating it to those who are to be the future guardians of the liberties of the country?[13]

Now my general point here has been to show the statesmanlike, that is, universal or comprehensive, stature and scope of Washington's perspective, from the time he became commander-in-chief during the Revolutionary War until his death at the close of the century. Washington's sustained viewpoint coherently links philosophical, religious, political, moral, military, commercial, and legal considerations across decades of public service for the long-range good of the United States and its people.

There are two serious objections to this assertion in my view. First is the claim that Washington incoherently attempted to combine an emphasis on modern property rights and commercial liberties with an expectation of civic duty more at home in ancient republics.[14] However a review of Washington's correspondence and political addresses will show no illusions about human nature and its infrequent self-sacrificing impulses. Rather, as we have seen, Washington always maintained that dutiful performance could only be counted on from the great majority of people as long as religious and moral obligations remained alive among them as well. Unless one is prepared to assert that commerce leads inexorably to atheism, I do not see that Washington can be justly accused of inconsistency on this score.[15]

The other serious criticism that might be raised in the context of my claim about Washington's concern for the general good is that he was in fact partisan.[16] This issue perhaps is best dealt with in a comparison of Washington with Hamilton and Jefferson.

In my view the issue of partisanship requires analysis about the differences *between* measures to establish and solidify constitutional arrangements (and their material preconditions) and measures that unambiguously favor some recognizable pattern of regional or short-run interests. It has been observed, for example, that once Jefferson left Washington's administration, Washington no longer made even a modest effort to balance Republican claims with Hamiltonian programs such as the plan for a national bank to monetize the war debts and centralize the country economically.[17] But, by itself, this is not evidence of mere partisanship if, in Washington's eyes, and on more objective grounds as well, Hamilton's financial program was essential to consolidation of the national union during a most critical, initial period.

This is a difficult and elusive point, but it is one that offers the theorist the infrequent chance to spread light rather than darkness on a practical matter. The question here, as I see it, is whether a consistently more long-range and comprehensive outlook can be called as equally partisan as a consistently shorter range and more particularly focused one. (This picture becomes even more complex if the general political goals differ, as between, say, liberal and socialist. But, in this case, the assumption would appear justified that Washington, Hamilton, and Jefferson were all agreed upon the general end of *stable* and enduring individual liberty.[18]) And I emphasize the qualification, "consistently long-range," because in any particular crisis attention to the shorter range consideration might be the more prudent from the standpoint of the ultimate preservation of the constitution or political system.

Now, in my view a perspective focused on the problem of maintaining and preserving a particular set of constitutional arrangements (and its material prerequisites—population, territory, resources, etc.) is simply not partisan in the sense that a more particular or sectional perspective must be. Moreover the former perspective would appear to be the central focus of all of Washington's efforts as commander-in-chief and then president. This was the reason why he hurried to leave public life as soon as the processes of politics became so partisan that *any* action to uphold the authority of the executive branch and preserve the union against foreign danger was seen as anti-Jeffersonian. It was not merely because Washington disliked being criticized (and villified), but because he was not interested in descending into the strife of diurnal politics; nor were his skills and character well suited to the arts of persuasion and alliance building among professional politicians. Rather his were the skills and traits that had developed in a military character with overarching responsibilities in times of major crisis.

Washington and Hamilton were suited to rescue or establish a system of authority from deterioration in the midst of chaos; having succeeded they really had no intelligent alternative but to retire to domestic life (unless the conditions that called forth their talents initially were to recur). But Washington understood this better, perhaps, than Hamilton, who was forced into this (happy) choice from necessity following his rapid fall from political influence in his home state of New York at the end of the century.[19] Perhaps by inclination Hamilton was no more "partisan" than Washington, but he was contentious and more ambitious for fame;[20] these two characteristics led him more surely into partisanship and partisan conflict. These reflections on Washington and Hamilton suggest that statesmen-founders generate political systems aiming at a general good from out of the midst of crises, when the more partisan-minded are weak and dependent and force it on the partisans who inexorably spend their subsequent energies attempting to undo their inheritance by reinterpreting it in the only way they can understand it—as a partisan act itself.

The case for Jefferson is more difficult from the standpoint of statesmanship *versus* partisanship, because of an added complexity—Jefferson's ambivalence toward things political. As is well known, his self-written epitaph makes no mention of his government service but records his contributions to causes of liberty and enlightenment. He seems, as has been suggested by John Dewey and others, to have seen himself more as a "scientist-legislator" than a "statesman-legislator."[21] Yet he also understood better than Hamilton and Washington how to organize large numbers of people on the basis of persuasion, and once in the highest office and thereafter, he took actions and offered explanations more characteristic of Hamilton or even Plato's "Stranger." First on the occasional need to go above the law, he wrote:

> A strict observance of the written law is doubtless *one* of the highest duties of a good citizen, but it is not *the highest.* The laws of necessity, of self-preservation, of saving our country when in danger, are of higher obligation.

> To lose our country by a scrupulous adherence to written law, would be to lose the law itself, with life, liberty, property, and all those who are enjoying them with us; thus absurdly sacrificing the end to the means.[22]

And in 1813, on the role of military service in civic education, he wrote:

> the necessity of obliging every citizen to be a soldier; this was the case with the Greeks and Romans, and must be that of every free State. . . . We must train and classify the whole of our male citizens and make military instruction a regular part of collegiate education.[23]

My point is not the banality that Jefferson had different emphases at different times (though it does seem that after his tenure as president he might have agreed more with certain ideas of Hamilton and Washington than when he was younger). Rather it is on this point that the case for statesmanship is more ambivalent for Jefferson, because he rejected on principle the idea that much good could be accomplished through political office other than creating the minimal conditions of peace and liberty, which would permit private society to flourish by developing the various arts and sciences. Furthermore, because Jefferson rejected the use of political office for the kinds of unification that Washington hoped to accomplish through his national university, or Hamilton through his centralized monetization programs, their actions must always seem partisan to Jefferson. The question for our analysis is whether Jefferson possessed the skills and perspective to have set firmly in place an enduring system of government as did Washington and Hamilton with the "blueprint" they received from the constitutional convention, or whether Jefferson could only operate within the authoritative structures they consolidated (and then alter them marginally). If the latter is true, as I believe it is, then Washington and Hamilton are more properly considered statesmen, if for no other reason than that they were more concerned with establishing a *state* and saw more clearly its importance for the things it made possible.

By the criteria I have laid out in evaluating Jefferson, it would also follow that Washington, in turn, is more properly labeled a statesman-founder than Hamilton, though it is perhaps pedantic to push this point too far. I simply have in mind that, owing perhaps to Hamilton's comparative youth and subordinate position during the war and in the new government (as well as perhaps to his admitted thirst for fame), Washington had the more comprehensive and balanced perspective on what was good for the country as a whole. If Hamilton understood more of the details of "Walpolean" finance[24] or had a wider reading acquaintance with philosophers of human nature such as David Hume,[25] this is not by itself evidence of the superiority of his political and moral *judgments* to those of Washington. And it is certainly not evidence of a superior ability to establish the authority of a new executive in a republican milieu instinctively hostile to it.[26] In fact, there is a case to be made that Hamilton could only deal in tandem with emphases—military, political, domestic, commercial, religious[27]— which Washington linked together coherently in a "public philosophy" (and in private life) for over forty years, which he then bequeathed to his country. As I have suggested above, this was not a contradictory amalgam of ancient and modern ideas but rather a version of Roman, especially Ciceronian,[28] republican principles about the importance for a public life of solid character, shored up by religious and moral obligations to oaths, contracts, the sanctity of private property,[29] and, above all, to a common bond of faith known as *res publica*.

SUMMARY

I have used Washington's life and career to illustrate the Platonic and Aristotelian idea that the statesman employs a comprehensive and universal art which guides the other arts and professions, directly or indirectly, for the common or general good and that one criterion of statesmanship is the ability to maintain this focus consistently and over time. I have used the case of Washington (and, to a lesser degree, Hamilton) to illustrate especially the difference between founding, firmly establishing, and maintaining a state, and conducting the daily (and more partisan[30]) business of politics. Next we take up the case of Abraham Lincoln to show how these two tasks converge in the event of a major constitutional crisis and, in general, as a constitutional system grows more democratic.

3

Abraham Lincoln

A MAJOR CRISIS IN THE LIFE OF A BODY POLITIC—WHETHER ECO-
nomic, military, constitutional, other, or all—calls for qualities of
statesmanship in political leaders that we have enumerated thus
far. Comprehensiveness of vision, from founding principles to a
grasp of the crisis of the moment; political skills of judgment,
persuasion, alliance building; and character traits of courage, decisiveness, and perseverance immediately come to mind. Inspection and critical evaluation of the ideas and actions of Abraham
Lincoln, in the decade leading up to and including the Civil War,
is useful in fleshing out and refining this list.

A major crisis, as Lenin was fond of observing, is always a time
of opportunity for the revolutionary minded or, we might add,
for the personally ambitious. An issue that presents itself immediately in assessing Lincoln's words and deeds from the standpoint
of statesmanship and the light they may shed on it as an art concerns Lincoln's motives or ultimate aims in doing so much to force
a confrontation between North and South over the slavery question. Was the first and foremost aim of this very talented and
perceptive man simply *to further the career* of a largely obscure
politician of humble origins named A. Lincoln? Or, in a grander
version, *to act out inexorably a cosmic destiny* at whatever human cost
or until he was stopped by events? Or, was Lincoln's first and
foremost aim *to achieve the common good* for the United States and
its future generations, as Lincoln understood it?

Said differently, the last question means to raise the issue of
whether Lincoln would have permitted the aim of the common
good of the Union to "override" the other two, if or when he
perceived a conflict among them. Much ink has been spilled in a
century and a half over this question,[1] yet there is more controversy here than Lincoln's actual words and deeds call for. In my
view Lincoln was so masterful at controlling words,[2] other men,

and to some extent, events, that *most of the time* he was able to make the three aims (of the preceding paragraph) converge, or at least not diverge too greatly to escape management. Hence what requires most to be judged in evaluating Lincoln as statesman is his vision of what was good for the people of the United States. Before addressing this question, let us explore further the matter of Lincoln's motives or ultimate ends.

That Lincoln came from humble circumstances and cultivated a local political career in the Whig Party is well known, as is the pronouncement of his Springfield, Illinois, law partner for seventeen years, William Herndon: "He was always calculating and planning ahead. His ambition was a little engine that knew no rest."[3] That Lincoln thought from early in his political career about really grand political questions is also evident in a much quoted paragraph from his "Lyceum speech" in 1837:

> Towering genius disdains a beaten path. . . . It scorns to tread in the footsteps of any predecessor. . . . It thirsts and burns for distinction; and, if possible, will have it, whether at the expense of emancipating slaves or enslaving free men.[4]

That Lincoln saw himself by the late 1850s as involved in events of political significance for the whole world (if not of *cosmic* significance) is also clear from public letters and private meditations:

> there has fallen upon me a task such as did not even rest upon the Father of his Country.[5]

> important crisis . . . involves, in my judgment, not only the civil and religious liberties of our own dear land, but in a large degree the . . . liberties of mankind in many countries through many ages.[6]

> In the present civil war, it is quite possible that God's purpose is something different from the purpose of either party. . . . I am almost ready to say that this is *probably true; that God wills this contest, and wills that it shall not end yet.* By his mere great power on the minds of the now contestants, He could either have saved or destroyed the Union without a human contest. Yet the contest began.[7]

In spite of Lincoln's clear belief in the grandeur of the events in which he was involved, there is also a Stoic side to his words (at least), which suggests that he was simply discovering and enacting a destiny that he would follow, whether it took him in or out of political office:

> I claim no insensibility to political honors; but today, could the Missouri restrictions be restored, and the whole slavery question be placed on the same old grounds . . . I would, in consideration, gladly agree that Judge Douglas should never be out, and I never in, an office so long as we both or either, live.

And on the same general point:

> I have never professed an indifference to the honors of official station. . . . Yet I have never failed . . . to recognize that in the Republican cause there is a higher aim than that of mere office.[8]

I believe there is no doubt of Lincoln's sincerity in these latter two pronouncements (nor that he was quite capable of happily returning to his Illinois law practice when no longer needed in public office), because this was apparently the only way that Lincoln could discover his destiny to his own satisfaction. To act contrary to his principles would, apparently, be to forego the opportunity to learn and perform what he was called to do. If he followed his principles to the utmost and still continued to live and be elected to public office, then he would not desist:

> I will make the South a graveyard rather than see . . . successful secession lose this government to the cause of the people and representative institutions.[9]

> I expect to maintain this contest until successful, or till I die, or am conquered, or my term expires, or Congress or the country forsake me.[10]

My general point here is that, as Lincoln's earlier cited meditation (that God probably had willed the conflict between North and South because He had the power to avoid it) suggests, theodicy may not have been Lincoln's most sophisticated area of reflection. That is, in the case of a man as politically talented as Lincoln, continued political success (in spite of an electoral loss or two) might not be the best indication of the rectitude of judgments and actions. This thought brings me back to my initial point about Lincoln's motivations: except to observe that Lincoln cultivated a conventional political career in order to be able to do some very

important things if called upon, the perspective of motives tells
us little, because whether Lincoln saw the importance of what he
must do in primarily political, or moral, or cosmic (even sacred)
terms, it is impossible to unravel if it was ever clear in Lincoln's
own mind.[11] Hence we are led back in investigating Lincoln's
statesmanship, for the light it may shed on the art of statesmanship, to a consideration of the political merits and consequences
of his ideas about what was good for the people of the United
States and, in turn (as he himself said), for those of other countries
as well.

The Political Vision of Abraham Lincoln

Lincoln's life and career present the theorist or spectator of
history with a fascinating spectacle—the *conjunction* of a sustained
and well considered vision or interpretation of the meaning of
America, the political potential to give this vision force, and a set
of critical circumstances that permitted this potential to actualize,
even flourish. If Lincoln was not exactly a founder, he was at the
least functioning at the general level of a founder by giving effect
to a creative interpretation of the meaning of his nation, which
expressly took it outside of the Constitution of 1787, back to the
ideas of one of Lincoln's admitted intellectual mentors, Thomas
Jefferson, as stated in the first paragraph of the Declaration of
Independence of 1776.

Said in theoretical terms Lincoln moved the nation and the
Union away from the (Roman and Norman) idea of the *overriding*
importance of procedures authoritatively enacted, toward the ancient Greek (and more democratic) idea that the laws of a constitution or regime are merely the expression of the essential, political
ideas of its most sovereign element. (As Aristotle says in *The Politics,* "The laws should be laid down, and all people do lay them
down, to suit the *politeia* and not the *politeia* to suit the laws."[12])
Now Lincoln makes it clear, time and time again, that the *essence*
of the American nation, in his view, from which its other and best
attributes derive is contained in the Jeffersonian (and Lockean)
idea that *all* men are created with equal natural or inalienable
rights to life, liberty, and the pursuit of happiness. Before pro-
ceeding with this account of Lincoln's political vision, let us look
at evidence of these initial ideas in Lincoln's own words.

First in support of the statement that Lincoln believed (unlike modern empiricists) that there was a fundamental or essential animating idea in the life of any body politic, and that in our case, it was the idea that *all* men were *created* equal:

> Without the *Constitution* and the *Union,* we could not have attained the result; but. . . . There is something back of these. . . . That something, is the principle of "Liberty to all."[13]

> Public opinion, on any subject always has a "central idea" from which all its minor thoughts radiate. The "central idea" in our political public opinion, at the beginning was, and until recently has continued to be, "the equality of men." . . . its constant working has been a steady progress toward the practical equality of all men.[14]

> Our government rests in public opinion. Whoever can change public opinion can change government practically just so much.[15]

Next what Lincoln understood this animating principle of the Declaration (not Constitution), which formed our nation, to mean in concrete terms:

> *The progress by which the poor,* honest, industrious and resolute *man raises himself,* that he may work on his own account, and hire somebody else, is that progress that human nature is entitled to . . . intended to be secured by those institutions under which we live, . . . *the great principle for which this government was really formed.*[16]

> There is no reason why the negro is not entitled to all the natural rights to life, liberty and the pursuit of happiness. I hold that he is as much entitled to these as the white man.[17]

Without distortion of Lincoln's ideas, I believe that what we have here from his own pen thus far suggests that in Lincoln's considered view, the Constitution and the Union are expressions of a more fundamental, animating idea which is the basis of the American nation and which was established "four score and seven years" before the Gettysburg Address of 1863, in the Declaration of Independence of 1776. This fundamental idea turns out to be a creative, Lincolnian modification of Jefferson's modification of Lockean natural rights to life, liberty, and property. But, although for Locke and Jefferson these are prepolitical rights inherent in all humanity by virtue of the right of self-preservation,[18] in Lincoln's transformation they have become the positive and ongoing goal of the Union, understood specifically to mean preservation of the hope for the poor (or latest wave of immigrants) to rise to the status of day laborers, thence to self-employed laborers or farmers, thence to employers themselves. This hope (or pursuit of happiness) to escape the status of permanent laborer[19] is what is promised in the American nation says Lincoln, and what has provided its industry and prosperity, thus far.

The next part of Lincoln's political vision for America is the idea that the Founders meant for these rights to apply to all men and proceeded in the hope and expectation that slavery would eventually be eliminated in the United States. Lincoln's various demonstrations of this point in the electoral debates of 1858 (with Douglas) are well known and include the following arguments, among others:

> The framers of the Constitution found the institution of slavery amongst their other institutions at the time. They found that by an effort to eradicate it, they might lose much of what they had already gained. They were obliged to bow to necessity. They gave power to Congress to abolish the slave trade at the end of twenty years. They also prohibited slavery in the territories where it did not exist.[20]

> by looking at the position in which our fathers originally placed it (slavery). . . . The public mind did rest in the belief that it was in the course of ultimate extinction.[21]

> I say . . . that three years ago there had never lived a man who ventured to assail it (the Declaration) in the sneaking way of pretending to believe it, and then asserting that it did not include the negro.[22]

Lincoln's basic argument goes on to establish that extension of the institution of slavery into the new territories of Kansas, Nebraska, New Mexico, and so on would indicate a symbolic approbation of what heretofore had been merely an evil tolerated as the price of union, and, hence, would amount to a repudiation, before ourselves and the whole world, of the animating principle of our existence as a nation, that *all* men are *created* equal. Furthermore Lincoln repeatedly asserted that the Dred Scott decision, the Kansas-Nebraska Act repealing the Missouri Compromise, and other evidence led him to *believe* in a conspiracy at the highest levels to nationalize slavery throughout the Union,[23] not merely by sending slave owners into new territories but eventually by way of a Supreme Court decision declaring "free state" constitutions unconstitutional. As Lincoln wrote a fellow Republican in December 1860, prior to assuming office:

> I am sorry any republican inclines to dally with Pop. Sov. *sic* of any sort. It acknowledges that slavery has equal rights with liberty, and surrenders all we have contended for. Once fastened on us as a settled policy, filibustering for all South of us, and making slave states of it, follow in spite of us, *with an early Supreme Court decision, holding our free-state Constitutions to be unconstitutional.*[24]

Lincoln made the same point in public addresses in Connecticut in 1860: "The overthrow of these constitutions will be demanded, and nothing left to resist the demand."[25]

Let us fill in our sketch of Lincoln's political vision for the United States by turning to his ideas about why secession was unacceptable as a response to the election of an (in Southern eyes) "abolitionist" president. Lincoln argued that secession amounted to anarchy[26] and anarchy the impending ruin of the whole country. Further such an outcome would spell the failure of the experiment in self-government that this country represented, and Lincoln was prepared to turn the South into a "graveyard" rather than see such a result.[27]

Finally as for his vision for freed slaves were a general emancipation ever possible, Lincoln appears to have gone through several phases, though none ever deviated from his claim that as human beings slaves had natural rights to live freely enough to consume the fruits of their own labor. As a young Whig politician, Lincoln appears to have favored citizenship as an eventual possibility;[28] then in the 1850s, as he came more into the national eye, he moved to a position that racial differences made suffrage and jury duty unfeasible,[29] requiring some sort of government-sponsored colonization, in the event of widespread emancipation.[30] Subsequently, after seeing the critical (in his view) contribution made to the cause of the Union military forces by over one hundred forty thousand black soldiers and sailors, Lincoln returned to the position of full political rights:

> I am responsible for it to the American people, to the Christian world, to history, and in my final account to God. Having determined to use

the negro as a soldier, *there is no way but to give him all the protection given to any other soldier.*[31]

ASSESSMENT OF LINCOLN'S STATESMANSHIP

In making an assessment of Lincoln's statesmanship for the light it may shed on the art of statesmanship, common sense requires some evaluation of the truth of his words, of his words against his deeds, and both words and deeds for their consequences.

Abraham Lincoln came indirectly to presidential power by making it impossible for Stephen A. Douglas to unite both northern and southern sentiment on the slavery question after their seven debates in the 1858 Illinois senatorial race. Lincoln did this by making explicit to the public the contradictions *between* Douglas's popular sovereignty doctrine for the territories *and* the 1857 Dred Scott decision that prohibited prohibition of slavery in the territories, both of which Douglas claimed to support. In particular Lincoln, as is well known, caused Douglas to alienate the South by asserting that a territory unfriendly to slavery could constitutionally keep it out in spite of Dred Scott, by simply refusing to provide for local police statutes (and enforcement) essential to the day-to-day existence of slavery ("the Freeport Doctrine").[32]

In the course of these tactical maneuvers, Lincoln also, as we have seen, expounded the broader argument that a "house divided against itself" could not stand and that the expansion of slavery into the territories would be a repudiation of the "central idea" of the American republic as Lincoln understood it (that all men are *created* equal), with dire consequences for the fate of liberty worldwide, starting with a likely Supreme Court decision declaring unconstitutional "free-state" constitutions. And he also made it clear to the South in 1859 that if elected President, he would *not* tolerate secession or repudiation of federal laws:

> So, if we constitutionally elect a President, and therefore you undertake to destroy the Union, it will be our duty to deal with you as old John Brown has been dealt with. We shall try to do our duty.[33]

Lincoln shepherded the nascent Republican Party during its initial period of electoral vulnerability, now cautioning prudence (e.g., silence in Illinois on the status of the controversial fugitive slave laws), now principled rigidity (e.g., no congressional compromise with Douglas's doctrine of "popular sovereignty").

We are surely required to ask: On how much of this was Lincoln right? How much did his talent and sustained will probably cause to happen? What would probably have happened otherwise? In my view, and in spite of the view of some twentieth-century historians that there were "natural limits to slavery,"[34] Lincoln was surely right that slavery would have extended into the territories if it was not legally prohibited (there is an interesting modern economic study showing that the rate of return on slave capital in the antebellum South ranged from 6 percent to 8 percent[35]), and he was certainly right that at a philosophic level extension of slavery into the territories would have been a symbolic repudiation of the first paragraph of the Declaration of Independence. Also his claim that Douglas's "popular sovereignty" doctrine, if it became the order of the day, would probably have been followed by a Supreme Court decision declaring unconstitutional "free-state" constitutions does not seem far-fetched in the light of the extraordinary conclusions of the Dred Scott decision, which repudiated as unconstitutional slavery prohibitions of even the Northwest Ordinance, unanimously passed by the first Congress of the United States. (And this outcome likely, in spite of Douglas's probably sincere protestations that such a court decision would amount to "moral treason;" Lincoln himself modified his view that Douglas was part of a conspiracy to nationalize slavery, suggesting that he was perhaps only its tool.[36])

On these various points Lincoln was, in my view, simply correct. The criticism of various contemporary historians that Lincoln precipitated a constitutional conflict over slavery, on the one hand, or that he should have moved more openly and less prudently to assert the natural and civil rights of the Black race on the other, are all simply variations on the theme of criticizing a political leader by assuming as givens the very achievements he struggled for and are usually predicated on some view of inevitable, historical progress working itself out through largely impersonal forces (but, certainly, not decisively through the work of "statesmen").

Now we enter a realm of events where Lincoln alone probably made the decisive difference (as did, we shall see, Churchill and De Gaulle, for their countries, in some respects during the Second World War). Even if Lincoln had not forced Douglas's hand in the 1858 senatorial debates and even if someone other than Lincoln had been elected president in 1860, it seems likely that some sort of armed conflict would have come over the slavery question, perhaps initiated by the North if Lincoln's prediction came true about an impending Supreme Court decision on the unconstituionality of "free-state" constitutions. (Buchanan, while still president, had railed against incipient Southern secession but said there was nothing he could do about it.) Without Lincoln's leadership would the conflict have ended in a complete northern victory? Or in the emancipation of all slaves and the passage of the thirteenth and fourteenth amendments after his death? And in a decisive, new democratic interpretation of the meaning of the United States (whether for good or ill), based on Lincoln's creative interpretation of Jefferson's words that "all men were created equal" to mean essentially continual improvement in the living conditions of the poor and less advantaged, rather than constitutionalism, per se? Jacksonian democracy, it is true, had elevated the image of the "common man," but it was Lincoln who gave the democratic claim gravity and respectability by creatively tracing it to the "fathers" and it was Lincoln who made it possible, as Woodrow Wilson would later say, "to believe in democracy."[37]

In my view the answer in the *first instance* is that Lincoln's sustained will and insightful judgments were the decisive element in the extent, duration, and outcome of the war, evidenced especially in his ability to raise and support an army through draft and income tax, in spite of the opposition of the Supreme Court; in his daring decision to incorporate over one hundred forty thousand Black soldiers and sailors into the Union effort;[38] and in the balance and good sense of his strategic judgment, which followed battlefield events closely and told him when to control generals like McClellan and when to empower generals like Grant. (Lincoln's letters to his generals are a fascinating study in their own right.) The answer in the *second instance* is that the legal pronouncements, which secured the North's achievements after the war, would have little effect in half the Union without the military outcome secured in the first instance. And the answer in the *third instance* is that while democratization (understood as growing equalization) of the American political system or regime would probably have come in some form over time, it might not have come in as free a form (following Tocqueville) as it did come; it might have occurred in a fragmented or smaller Union, and it would not have been framed in expressly Lincolnian language and ideas.

It is in this last instance—the meaning of the American system—that Lincoln the statesman made his greatest, and perhaps most problematic, achievement. Let us rehearse it. The preceding pages have tried to show that by throwing his political talents into a sustained, principled conflict with the southern doctrine that slavery was not merely an evil to be tolerated but in fact a "positive good." Abraham Lincoln entered into, deepened, and resolved for the most part a major conflict between North and South by raising and directing a victorious army in support of a "creative" but plausible new interpretation of the meaning of the American nation. In brief Lincoln's view was that this nation dated from the Declaration of Independence, not the Articles of Confederation or the Constitution of 1787, and that its "central idea" was the Jeffersonian phrase that all men are created equal, understood *not* as a Lockeanlike observation of the prepolitical, natural rights of humanity but rather as a positive goal to be pursued, understood first and foremost as the creation and preservation of economic opportunity for the poor and oppressed in the United States and throughout the world.

Now this was a possible interpretation of the meaning of the United States, though probably not the one that would have been shared by a majority of the Founders so revered in Lincoln's oratory. Their view, on the whole, would probably have been closer to that of Lincoln's older contemporary, James Fenimore Cooper, who, writing in 1838, argued that "We the people" in the preamble to the Constitution clearly meant to its framers the people as organized in entities called "states" and represented at the constitutional convention by their delegates:

The notion that the *people* of the United States, in the popular sense of the word, framed the government, is contrary to fact. . . . The constitution of the United States was formed by a convention composed of delegates elected by the different states . . . the constitution of the United States was framed by the states then in existence, as communities, and not by the body of the people of the Union, or by the body of the people of the states, as has been sometimes contended. . . . In a political sense, the people means those who are vested with political rights, and in this particular instance, the people vested with political rights were the constituencies of the several states. . . . "We the *people*," as used in the preamble of the constitution, means merely, "We the *constituencies* of the several states."[39]

The views of the Founders in the main were probably closer to those of Lincoln's skeptical mentor, Thomas Jefferson, that is, that the religious, ethical, and economic differences which separated the peoples of the various states were sufficiently great *that what bound them together* could never be a single, substantive good to be pursued as the meaning of the nation[40] but rather the constitution understood as a social compact among the states (explicit, for example, in the various secession and dissolution declarations of the southern states), laying out rules and procedures for an extended, federal, republican government, with certain liberties secured against the *national* government.

Even this more "constitutional" view of the *meaning* of the United States does not permit secession as part of its constitutional procedures, nor could any president remain true to the oath of office and permit it without a conflict. (Still, as some Southerners have never ceased to observe, Lincoln's particular understanding of a more pervasive Union organized around a single "central idea" did require extensive use of armed force to gain acceptance and, thereby, raises doubts about the accuracy of any subsequent reference to the Constitution of 1787 as a "social compact," which arose from the consent of the governed.[41]) Suffice it to say, for our purposes here, Lincoln preserved the Union by employing both coercive and persusasive means, gave it a new interpretation, generated (posthumously) the constitutional authorization to make his vision of the meaning of America the dominant one, and, also, eliminated the indisputably evil institution of chattel slavery in the United States of America. How are we to judge his achievements from the perspective of "statesmanship?"

Alexis de Tocqueville had argued (with remarkable accuracy) from his observations of America and France during the 1830s, that growing equality of conditions among humanity worldwide was *the* political future; that the issue was now simply whether that equality was to be free and diverse, or oppressive and uniform; and that no political movement or leader could *sustain* power without paying tribute to the idea of equality—even tyranny would now come in the name of equality, Tocqueville predicted.[42] It can, with fairness I believe, be said that Lincoln forced the South into acceptance of antislavery ideas which were healthy for the future of liberty and formal equality worldwide, and, in this sense, his goal was a worthy one.[43] But by formalizing and sanctioning such a substantive and economic understanding of the meaning of America (i.e., the *primacy* of economic opportunity) at the expense of a more formal and transcendent understanding of our constitutional arrangements, Lincoln indirectly provided support rather than resistance to the widespread, cynical, and plausible view that the meaning of America was merely the pursuit of wealth, a concern Lincoln himself pondered obliquely, writing in 1864:

> As a result of the war, corporations have been enthroned and an era of corruption in high places will follow, and the money power of the country will endeavor to prolong its reign by working upon the prejudices of the people until . . . the Republic is destroyed.[44]

But, more importantly against Lincoln, in my view, his vision and actions contributed to the millennialist tendency already prevalent in New England and the midwest especially, to fuse the sacred and the profane (hence the importance of the economic realm and economic expansion[45]) in a way that, Washington, for example, would never have done. And this is not merely for the reason, as has been suggested, that Washington simply viewed religion for its utility in securing national morality,[46] but because Washington knew the difference between the sacred and the profane and consistently maintained greater clarity about it than did Lincoln. However, it would require a more explicitly millennialist "statesman," Woodrow Wilson (our next subject), to deal effectively with the problem of Lincoln's "corporations" by democratizing and millennializing the *meaning* of the United States still further.

General Conclusion

We noted at the outset that consideration of Lincoln's achievements would allow us to refine and expand our understanding of the art of statesmanship. The major point to be made here is the tendency of a fundamental crisis in the life of a body politic to call into power individuals with statesmanlike qualities. That is, because a major crisis or explicit contradiction in the life of any people calls into question *some* of their fundamental beliefs and principles, it requires a statesmanlike breadth and depth of vision and concentration to search outside the present crisis to its origins for solutions and know how to bridge from the one to the other.[47] Hence resolution (short of anarchy) of a major crisis such as the slavery question requires the conjunction in a single individual of historical and ethical insight with qualities of practical judgment necessary to indicate in advance of action how much of the "new" a people can tolerate at the moment, how much of the "new" can be reconstructed from original materials, and so on. Within these margins, as we have seen in the case of Lincoln, there is room for creative interpretation, which may influence the directions and may set the horizons for the public energies of a people for generations to come.

Several qualities of Lincoln's leadership were not only important in managing a wartime crisis but are illustrative, as well, of qualities set forth in Plato's *Statesman* in this book's first chapter. Lincoln's ability to inspire unified convictions on the war effort among a northern and border-state alliance of both Republicans and Democrats with varying views on the slavery question is remarkable. This achievement was owed, in part, to Lincoln's oratory, in particular his extraordinary use of practical metaphor, parable, religious imagery, and poetic cadence to simplify and drive home abstract points for a democratic audience (and their newspaper reporters) averse to fine logical distinctions in public discourse. (It even has been suggested that the South might have won the war if Lincoln were its leader rather than the aloof Jefferson Davis.[48]) Part of this achievement was also due to Lincoln's understanding of the business of alliance building among diverse groups and his willingness to balance requirements of political patronage (to keep the war effort going) with those of military expertise, for example, in the appointment of his generals.

Lincoln's relationship as political leader to the art of strategy perhaps goes beyond the idea of Plato's Stranger, that is, the statesman must know merely when to set this art in motion. Lincoln was an extraordinary wartime leader[49] (exhibiting qualities equaled perhaps only by Churchill), capable of tailoring military means to political ends, as the political end of the war evolved from suppressing a rebellion to the total destruction of southern forces as a step in the emancipation of all slaves. Lincoln actively engaged in the general direction of some campaign movements (especially around Washington) until he found a military commander whom he thought competent (U. S. Grant) to grasp and carry out his general war aims; after that he withdrew to a position more aptly characterized as political direction of the war.

A final, general issue for analysis in Lincoln's career, I have just indicated under the rubric of "millennialism."[50] I understand this to mean the attempted overcoming of the tension between Christ's teachings and pagan politics (described in the first chapter of this book) by employing political means to modify radically (even eliminate) the fundamental structure of political reality itself. This is a dubious development from the standpoint of the art of statesmanship, because it risks blurring the boundaries and limits of what can be intelligently accomplished in political actions and threatens to make politics into something greater than it can be (whether in the explicit name of politics or not). However, because I think the label of millennialist far more aptly fits our next subject, Woodrow Wilson, than Lincoln,[51] I leave a discussion of this problem to the conclusion of a consideration of Wilson's accomplishments.

4

Woodrow Wilson

INSPECTION OF THE ACADEMIC AND POLITICAL CAREER OF WOOD-
row Wilson—political scientist, governor, president, world
leader—is useful in our analysis of statesmanship for several disparate reasons in addition to the obvious ones. On the obvious
side, Wilson was clearly an articulate, persuasive, political leader
of his party and his nation, a successful legislative leader vis-à-vis
the Congress until the last two years of his second term,[1] and a
world leader who articulated a vision of international cooperation
that has grown more actual in the years since the Second World
War.

I wish to explore his career as an academic and political leader
for the light it may shed on the art of statesmanship in the modern world from three less obvious perspectives. The first is the
relationship of statesmanship to ideas and theories of political life;
the second involves skills necessary for fundamental alteration of
a constitution or political system from within during relatively
normal (rather than revolutionary) times; and the third involves
the issue of millennialist reform, or the use of political means to
alter the fundamental structure of political reality (usually in the
name of the progressive elimination of evil on earth), and its consequences for the art of statesmanship.

First is the relationship of ideals and general theory to political
practice. Consider in this context the following statement by a
contemporary political theorist:

> Perhaps the highest task of . . . statesmanship is to govern, the relation
> of political life to thought. The genius of the American regime assigns
> this highest task of statesmanship to the people themselves. . . . This
> means that the character of the people is called upon to stand in place
> of wisdom.[2]

This statement was perhaps not made without mild irony, but
it is a statement that Wilson would probably have accepted in

private at least (in his public oratory, as we shall see, he likely would have equated the "character of the people," properly guided, with wisdom). Certainly Wilson, both as a political science educator and as a political leader, was expressly concerned with the relationship of thought, ideas, and moral principles to political life; in particular he was concerned with using ideas to effect changes in public opinion, which, when institutionalized in university curricula and, in turn, in governmental policies, would transform deep-seated social and political practices. Here is Wilson, the political scientist, on this very subject in 1887:

> Whoever would effect a change in modern constitutional government must first educate his fellow-citizens to want some change. That done, he must persuade them to want the change he wants. He must first make public opinion willing to listen and then see to it that it listens to the right things.
>
> The bulk of mankind is rigidly unphilosophical, and nowadays the bulk of mankind votes. A truth must become not only plain but also commonplace before it will be seen by the people who go to their work very early in the morning.[3]

How Wilson viewed the exact relation between himself and the "public mind" or public opinion at various stages in his career is difficult to know exactly. Certainly by the time of the 1912 presidential campaign, he spoke in his public addresses of the *feelings* of the "common man" as a guide for political leaders:

> Everything I know about history . . . has confirmed me in the conviction that the real wisdom of human life is compounded out of the experiences of ordinary men.

> Nobody who cannot speak the common thought, who does not move by the common impulse, is the man to speak for America, or for any of her future purposes.[4]

Although the emphasis is different between the professional writing and the campaign addresses twenty-five years later, there is no clear contradiction. Wilson still clearly believed that "wherever public opinion exists it must rule"; he was simply trying to influence it by articulating what it was vaguely feeling and by providing the political program to give expression and effect to those *feelings*.

The theme that he was a conduit for the "public mind" recurs often in Wilson's thoughts once he became president and appears to be something he sincerely believed. Here is a representative instance:

> remember that we laid down fourteen points. They were not my points. *In every one of them I was conscientiously trying to read the thought of the people of the United States,* and after I uttered those points I had every assurance . . . that they did speak the moral judgment of the United States and not my single judgment.[5]

Here is the same idea more generally stated in a diary entry:

> I *receive* the opinions of the day, I do not *conceive* them. . . . *Why may not the present age write, through me, its political autobiography?*[6]

Moreover these later views were generally consistent with Wilson's earlier academic views on the role of the president, though with less emphasis on the originality of the individual leader's views:

> The President represents . . . the party's . . . vital link or connection with the thinking nation. . . . *If he rightly interpret the national thought* and boldly insist upon it, he is irresistable. . . . A President whom it trusts can not only lead it, but form it to his own views.[7]

Ultimately, as we shall see in our discussion of Wilson's millennialism, he may have thought that the source of correct political ideas was a proper reading of the direction of history, something the people could "feel" and a leader like Wilson could articulate for them. (It has even been suggested that Wilson saw himself in something like a "gnostic union" with the people of the United States.[8]) But my general point here is that Wilson clearly believed in the power of ideas and moral ideals to unify a majority of the electorate dedicated to a particular political vision and that a part of statesmanship was to articulate and lay out a vision of social and political reform to galvanize the nation behind it and give it effect. What was Wilson's vision (a term he himself often used) of political reform, as it evolved over an academic and political career of four decades? In spite of tactical alterations (e.g., on the role of Congress in its relation with the presidency), it has remarkable continuity and consistency, starting with Wilson's "solemn convenant" with his Princeton classmate, Charles Talcott, to "school all our powers and passions for the work of establishing the principles we held in common" to form a new political sentiment and party in the country:

> I believe . . . that if a band of young fellows . . . should raise a united voice in . . . periodicals, great or small, . . . they could gain access . . . to a position of prominence and acknowledged authority in the public prints, and so in the public mind, a long step would have been taken towards the formation of such a new political sentiment and party as the country stands in such need of.[9]

What was the political vision Wilson wished to promulgate? In brief it consisted in the necessity of overcoming the checks and balances of the "outdated" federal constitution of 1787, to unify power behind democratically chosen party leaders, who would reform government and use it efficiently to curtail the power and influence of a corporate oligarchy, while pursuing legislation and policies designed to aid the common man, as well as contribute to the progressive *redemption* of the entire world through the providentially guided leadership of the United States. Let us follow Wilson's reasoning on the various facets of this vision.

First is Wilson's consistent view of the constitution of 1787:

> We are the first Americans to . . . ask whether the Constitution is still adapted to serve the purposes for which it was intended. . . . The noble Charter . . . of 1787 is still our Constitution, but it is now our *form of government* rather in name than in reality.[10]

> The trouble with the (Federalist) theory is that government is not a machine, but a living thing . . . accountable to Darwin, not to Newton. . . . *No living thing can have its organs offset against each other, as checks, and live.* . . . All that progressives ask . . . is . . . to interpret the Constitution according to Darwinian principle.[11]

In concrete terms this meant that Wilson denigrated deference to the constitution and to established political, economic, and social elites to urge concentration and magnification of national power (over state and local power) through the various proposals of the progressives—expanded interpretations of the commerce clause to include production; a national income tax, a Federal Reserve System, and strong regulatory legislation; an expanded suffrage generally and in the election of senators particularly; and so on. All of this was to be in the interest of the common or

average man, as articulated and defined by enlightened, liberally
educated elites, who read his feelings and as implemented by a
new class of efficient and "scientifically neutral" administrators. It
also meant, initially for Wilson, the need for a parliamentary-
style cabinet government to overcome the fragmentation of the
congressional committee system and subsequently (after the
Spanish-American War) the need for a strong and vigorous presidential leader to guide progressive reforms through the national
legislature. In time, as we shall see, Wilson's vision also flowed into
the international realm, to urge a revolution in the way states dealt
with one another.

Now all of this clearly signified a revolution or fundamental
change in the American system of government, one that might
be viewed as institutionally empowering democratic majorities
through the conduit of strong, national leaders acting in their
name through the use of government, a development glimpsed
in the wartime leadership of Abraham Lincoln and forestalled
by Supreme Court decisions during the last four decades of the
nineteenth century.[12]

How did Wilson bring all of this about or at least contribute
decisively to its implementation? Said more generally, how do the
requirements of statesmanship directed toward peaceful but major transformation of a political system differ from those of a
founding following the use of arms? The short answer is that the
statesmen must rely more heavily on the use of ideas to change
attitudes, first those of elites who educate public opinion and then
those of the mass of citizens (whose modified views can then be
used to pressure elites still more). An examination of Wilson's
strategy in this regard is revealing not only for an understanding
of his own rise to power and subsequent achievements but also
for confirming the power of statesmanlike oratory (whether in
esoteric academic literature, in the classroom, or in campaign addresses) in bringing about political change.

Wilson's strategy for political transformation of the United
States has been critically and systematically analyzed in great detail by Paul Eidelberg in his book, *A Discourse on Statesmanship:
The Design and Transformation of the American Polity*. Eidelberg's
thesis is that the twentieth century witnessed the transformation
of our eighteenth-century system of mixed government "into one
in which the democratic principle gained complete ascendency"
and that it was in the era of Woodrow Wilson (rather than Jeffer-

son, Jackson, or Lincoln) that there occurred "the intellectual ascendency of democracy, an ascendency carried to *material* completion under Franklin Roosevelt and the New Deal."[13] In my view Eidelberg occasionally becomes inaccurate when assessing Wilson's part in this transformation by stating as certain what is problematic, for example, the *effects* of Wilson's ideas on the American people. But Eidelberg's analysis of the *logical implications* of Wilson's ideas is masterful, and because I do not wish unfairly to claim credit for it, I shall simply summarize it for the light it sheds on the requirements of a rhetorical strategy for bringing about democratic conditions.

Eidelberg deals with changes in the emphasis of Wilson's ideas over four decades, not by seeing a fundamental shift after Wilson joined the Progressives (and changed his ideas about figures such as William Jennings Bryan[14]) but by treating Wilson's public rhetoric as separate from his more esoteric and professional teaching in academic journals and books. Wilson's public teaching, as interpreted by Eidelberg, emphasized "the wisdom of the common man," and leadership which could read and feel his (incipient) thoughts in order to serve him, through reform and use of government for his convenience and prosperity. Wilson's academic and more esoteric teaching emphasized the wisdom of experts and scientists ("the many, the people . . . are selfish, ignorant, timid, stubborn or foolish"[15]) in administering a government for "the many." Both aspects of this "teaching," however, required a rhetorical strategy that would gradually undermine reverence and respect for the established order while generating a sustained and moderate passion for change (not violent revolution).

Wilson's basic vision included, then, the requirement for strong leadership that would read the feelings of the average or common man, articulate them in a political program, overcome the residual (since the Civil War) checks and balances of the old federal system in the interest of centralized power to give this vision effect, and, eventually, extend this vision into the international realm to overcome traditional balance of power politics.

We have already seen how Wilson began undermining the deference to the Constitution of 1787 by emphasizing time after time its irrelevance to the present age and its problems, but Wilson's rhetorical strategy, as analyzed by Eidelberg, also included undermining deference to the rich and powerful. This project included remarks to create the impression that those with wealth and economic influence owed it primarily to chance, not merit:

> Most of us are average men; very few of us rise, *except by fortunate accident,* above the general level of the community about us.[16]

> As a university president, I learned that the men who dominate our manufacturing processes could not conduct their business for twenty-four hours without the assistance of the experts with whom the universities were supplying them.[17]

The implications of these observations of Wilson's are drawn out by Eidelberg:

> Having had revealed to them the fortuitous character of worldly success, hence the groundlessness of their deferential attitude toward men of wealth and power, the average man was more susceptible to the Wilsonian persuasion that justice requires government to equalize conditions. Why, indeed, should government protect the few whose success is to be attributed to "fortunate accident" rather than their own merit?[18]

Another feature of Wilson's rhetoric or oratory (besides its generation of anger and resentment toward the established order), according to Eidelberg, was its manipulation of the feelings of compassion and self-pity among his audience: "I want to see a government rooted also in the pains and suffering of mankind. I want to see a government which is not pitiful but full of human sympathy."[19] Eidelberg then draws out the implications of Wilson's emphasis on the "politics of compassion":

> Consider the psychological effects and political consequences of explaining privilege in terms of chance as opposed to merit. Clearly, such a teaching cannot but engender among the "underprivileged" resentment on the one hand, and self-pity on the other. But as any student of human nature knows, there is hardly a more effective way of emasculating an individual and gaining power over his will than by evoking self-pity. This may be done by blaming others or bad luck for his plight and by indulging him with sympathy.[20]

Eidelberg attempts to make these aspects of Wilson's rhetoric clearer by contrasting it with Teddy Roosevelt's rhetoric in the "new nationalism," noting that

Roosevelt did not exalt the common man; he spoke less of freedom and more of men's duties; his public teaching about equality of opportunity more clearly exemplifies distributive or proportionate justice; and he did not wish to eliminate monopolies but to regulate them.[21]

Finally Eidelberg summarizes the import of Wilson's private and public teaching: "In short, compassion and intelligence are to join in the task of alleviating the human condition by equalizing all conditions,"[22] through the medium of government regulation. On the role of government, Eidelberg cites a relevant paragraph from Wilson's academic work, *The State:*

> Not license of interference on the part of government, only strength and adaptation of regulation. The regulation that I mean is not interference: it is equalization of conditions, in so far as possible, in all branches of endeavor.[23]

In my view Eidelberg is successful in showing that Wilson had a long-range vision for fundamental change of the American political system (extending back to his days as a student at Princeton), a major part of which required the use of political rhetoric (even in scholarly works) to change the ideas and shift the loyalties of opinion-making elites as a step on the way to changing mass opinion and to actual political power. And although it is true that Wilson swam with the tide of progressivism and philosophic pragmatism, he also did much to articulate their explicit meaning in the realm of politics and policy and give it practical force. But Woodrow Wilson, the self-described conduit for the feelings of the "common man," was the articulator of more than simply pragmatic progressivism for the convenience and prosperity of the "plain people." Wilson was also at the forefront of what has been called "millennialism," and to evaluate Wilson's statesmanship and its consequences for the United States, and, more generally, for the art of statesmanship, we must move outside of a discussion of Wilson's efforts to legitimate increasing democratization in the name of progress, to the deeper and broader basis and understanding of this progress. A good point of departure for analysis of this aspect of Wilson's statesmanship is American historian Ernst Lee Tuveson's classic work, *Redeemer Nation: The Idea of America's Millennial Role.*

Tuveson defines millennialism as "the belief that history, under divine guidance, will bring about the triumph of Christian principles, and that a holy utopia will come into being" and suggests that some version of this millennialist doctrine has probably been dominant among English-speaking Protestants since the late seventeenth century.[24] The force of Tuveson's book is in showing, through extensive quotation, that this outlook characterized *mainstream* (not fringe or extremist) Protestant thought from Jonathan Edwards to Woodrow Wilson and was especially instrumental in mobilizing Northern sentiment and energy during the Civil War. This outlook was asserted again and again in both nineteenth-century academic (e.g., *Princeton Review, Presbyterian Quarterly Review*) and popular literature and in its particular American version, included the view that America was to be the locus of God's Kingdom on earth and that divine Providence was working itself out through the medium of the American people. Here is Tuveson's summary of a typical statement of American millennialism, from an 1858 *Harper's New Monthly Magazine* article entitled, "Providence in American History":

> The author asserts that the fundamentals of American democracy have developed from the idea of a Kingdom of God on earth. . . . The author . . . expresses a widespread conviction when he says that "the American Constitution has a moral meaning, a sacredness, over and above what political science and civil compacts can ever give to the organic law of a commonwealth."
> In America, moreover, the chosen people has found its appointed theater.[25]

Tuveson goes on to show that Woodrow Wilson (the son of a Presbyterian minister) came out of this tradition, stayed within it (especially during his time at Princeton), and was a forceful articulator of its outlook, especially during his frantic campaigning to gain ratification of the treaty for the League of Nations, when he expressly began to say that it was America's destiny to redeem the world.[26] Yet Tuveson's claim is not really controversial with regard to Wilson and is acknowledged by Wilson scholars who are not even primarily interested in the millennialist side of Wilson's personality. Here is a remarkably candid statement by the author of a recent book concerned primarily with showing Wilson as a great legislative leader:

> In his argument that patriotism is "the duty of religious men," in fact, he turned orthodox Calvinism, which sought a political order that

would protect true religion, upside down. Believing that Christianity required service to others, Wilson shared the conviction common among late nineteenth-century American Protestants that God's kingdom was evolving on earth, especially in the United States. *"We are to be an instrument in the hands of God to see that liberty is made secure for mankind,"* he said in 1917, and he believed that his own role was to be an evangelist of that plan, both at home and around the world.[27]

Before turning to an analysis of the significance of this for Wilson's political leadership and for the art of statesmanship in general, let us look at several instances of this view in Wilson's own words. Here is a remarkable piece of argumentation from the speech alluded to by Tuveson in the quotation above, which goes beyond Wilson's immediate rhetorical purpose of uniting domestic divisions for the coming war effort and moves explicitly into the realm of theodicy (where it could have easily backfired as a mere rhetorical strategy). Speaking in 1917 to surviving Confederate veterans of the Civil War, Wilson said:

> we now at last see why this great Nation was kept united for we are beginning to see the great world purpose which it was meant to serve . . . (and which at the time of the Civil War) we were incapable of conceiving as we tried to work things out with our short sight. . . . And now that we see ourselves part of a Nation united, powerful . . . we know the great ends which God in His mysterious Providence wrought through our instrumentality. . . . we are to be an instrument in the hands of God to see that liberty is made secure for mankind.[28]

The implication here is that if the American people are the instrument of Providence on earth and Woodrow Wilson is the leader who can give expression to their common thoughts and feelings, then it is Woodrow Wilson who is the indispensable agent in this providential plan—but more of this later. Here is another piece of Wilsonian reasoning on this same point, from less troubled times, set forth in a well-publicized address entitled "The Bible and Progress," delivered in 1911 at Denver, Colorado:

> America is not ahead of other nations of the world because she is rich. Nothing makes America great except . . . her ideals, except her acceptance of those standards of judgment which are written large upon these pages of revelation. America has all along claimed the distinction of setting this example to the civilized world. . . .
> This is the reason that the Bible has stood at the back of progress.[29]

And, finally, in one of Wilson's last pieces, after his illness and retirement, he wrote:

> The supreme task, which is nothing less than the salvation of civiliza-
> tion now faces democracy. . . . we call ourselves a Christian civilization,
> and a Christian conception of justice must be higher. It must include
> . . . a willingness to forego self-interest in order to promote the wel-
> fare, happiness, and contentment of others and of the community as
> a whole.[30]

Now the issue for our analysis concerns the consequences of Wilson's millennialism for the future practice of statesmanship. Tuveson characterizes millennialism as the (very un-Augustinian) attempt to build the Kingdom of God on earth through incremental elimination of evil throughout the world. Another author describes Wilson's "civil religion" as that of an "idealist" in the sense in which the English political theorist, T. H. Green, defined him: "One who seeks to 'enact God in the world' by the pursuit of ideals not given in experience."[31] I have earlier described millennialism as the misguided attempt to use political and other means to alter fundamentally the structure of political reality. The issue in this context for assessing Wilson's political achievements involves arriving at some judgments about which of Wilson's ideas, actions, and policies were the direct result of this sustained outlook and about the overall effect of this Wilsonian legacy on the politics of the United States and the world.

To begin with Wilson's idea of democracy would appear to have been informed by a religious teaching that he inherited concerning the end of time, when, "the last shall be first," and the downtrodden and oppressed will be elevated. That is, Wilson's idea of democracy was not that of rule by and for the whole but rule by the (leaders of) "common men" over any sort of privilege and privileged person. Wilson repeatedly stated that the standard of the political future (for the whole world) was the "moral" outlook of the common or average or plain people:

> The fortunes of mankind are now in the hands of the plain people
> of the whole world. . . . a body that constitutes a great democracy.
> They expect their leaders to speak their thoughts and no private pur-
> pose of their own. They expect their representatives to be their ser-
> vants. *We have no choice but obey their mandate.*[32]

Not only does Wilson's idea of democracy appear to be exactly what Madison called a "majority faction," but in its elevation of the average over the excellent and meritorious, it does represent (as the basis for policies, laws, constitutional interpretations, and amendments) an attempt to "enact ideals not given in experience." Moreover it produced dubious side effects for the very thing that Wilson entered politics to protect from the influence of a stifling, corporate oligarchy—the intergrity of the individual conscience.[33] Although Wilson occasionally used phrases about "an infinite individual variety," the logical thrust of his emphasis on equality of conditions was, as Eidelberg has observed, to elevate the species over the individual:

> The logic of Wilson's public teaching denied the right of any individual to enjoy any privileges whatever. Obliterated as a consequence, was the distinction between the possession and the exercise of a right, hence the distinction between man *qua* species and man *qua* individual. Under a dispensation characterized by the equalization of conditions, all men *qua* individuals would exercise the rights they possessed *qua* species. The species would thus be elevated above the individual— but under the facade of individuality.[34]

Now there was no doubt a threat to the integrity of individual choice for large numbers of people in the concentration of corporate wealth and power which Wilson set himself to oppose. But (as thinkers such as Tocqueville, Mill, and Nietzsche had observed) there was also a threat to individuality, and perhaps a more spiritual one, in egalitarian societies of the kind that Wilson attempted to bring about. The evidence here obliges one to conclude that Wilson's vision of democracy was not merely the expression of an effort to re-right the balance of the republic following the rise and growth of a plutocracy since the Civil War but rather to effect a fundamental transformation of the American way of life based on what Tuveson calls Wilson's millennialist program. As I shall suggest subsequently, Wilson's vision went too far outside of what can be achieved within political experience, with dubious consequences for both a politics of civility and for the expression of the religious faith that Wilson rightly saw as the moral basis of an ethics of individual conscience.[35]

A second dubious effect of Wilson's particular conception of democracy as the embodiment of the average and plain man's will, as articulated by leaders in touch with his feelings, has been a reduced and less comprehensive sense of political responsibility among individual citizens and voters. This has come about, in part, as a result of Wilson's rhetorical and pedagogic strategy to undermine deference to the constitution and to social elites as part of a program to check the influence of big business and the political establishment of the time. The effect has been to efface a sense of responsibility for the *whole* country among many individuals citizens, who have, since the presidency of Wilson (and that of Franklin D. Roosevelt as well), been taught to think expressly in class-oriented terms except in times of emergency. Absent in the rhetoric of Wilson is an emphasis on the political arts as a basis for the moderate reconciliation of differences among the various interests of the country. Rather the emphasis in the Wilsonian inheritance is on a *vision* of what is best for the average or plain people, explicitly identified as democracy or the good of the whole people—one articulated by benign, enlightened leaders such as Wilson (what Croly called "saints" or "heroes") and driven by an intense, moral exertion to reform and redeem the world. By speaking in the name of the "plain people" and trying to enact "their" will in history for them, it would seem that Wilson actually encouraged their moral and spiritual dependency rather than their independence, for Wilson's leadership nourished rather than discouraged the tendency of the "average man" to be one-sided rather than catholic in his outlook (by identifying with other "average men"). It also took away incentive for individual achievement by bestowing rights upon them (through national police powers) *qua* species rather than as individuals and by denigrating the idea of even earned privileges. Wilson's leadership removed from them the burden of the responsibility to be capable of articulating their own interests, by representing Wilson himself as the spokesman who could do it for them and through whom they could write their "political autobiography." Furthermore, by his rhetorical cultivation of the sentiments of compassion and self-pity, he made his audiences softer rather than harder anytime they were not united in some great, collective moral exertion. And, finally, by emphasizing the idea that leaders were, in turn, the mere "servants" of the plain people who could "feel" better than they the direction or spirit of the age (or of history), Wilson absolved even elected leaders from the responsibility to be leaders while in office; they were now merely trustees or conduits of the collective will as directed by providence.

Another dubious political effect of Wilson's millennialist views occurred in the realm of foreign policy and international affairs. Much of the drive behind Wilson's vision of a new international order came from his desire to eliminate reliance upon the "balance of power" strategy for stability among states (Wilson was not interested in stability, per se, but in "progress"), as well as other aspects of traditional statecraft such as secret arrangements, and the use of armed force in pursuit of national interests (including retaliations). All of this was clearly an attempt to enact ideals that were not heretofore "given in experience," and we need to inspect this aspect of Wilson's vision for the world closely in this regard. Is the absoluteness of Wilson's international aims explainable by a belief in the immanent arrival of an age when "the wolf shall be a guest of the lamb, and the leopard shall lie down with the kid"? Were Clemenceau's descriptions of Wilson as one who thought himself a new messiah not mere rhetorical exaggerations?

Our concern here is to assess Wilson's vision for a League of Nations to replace the old balance of power system and eliminate the causes of war in the context of its consequences for the art of statesmanship. As Wilson's critics on the left and right have pointed out for decades, his actual programs and policies, even the Fourteen Points, were a blend of idealism and American self-interest, containing contradictions such as the tension between the goal of world interdependence and the requirement for unilateral (U.S.) intervention, or between a peace treaty to eliminate the causes of war and also punish Germany, or between a world bent on cooperation and a world of states expressing their various national "self-determinations."

However it is Wilson's way of viewing his international efforts (including U.S. entry into the war), and the arguments he used to justify and gain support for them, which have been his most enduring legacy to the United States and which concern us most in an analysis of his statesmanship. For it is clear that Wilson saw his proposals as steps in the fundamental transformation of the system of intercourse among states, a transformation to enact in actual experience practices so idealistic and extreme as to preclude realistic expectation of success. Like his first secretary of state, William Jennings Bryan, Wilson meant to enact in history an ethics for states predicated on a religious belief in the primacy and overriding importance (for all seasons) of the individual conscience. As Wilson said explicitly in a public address in 1916, explaining the idea of the League: "It is clear that nations must in the future be governed by the same high code of honor that we demand *of individuals.*"[36]

This code meant not only that all international dealings were to be open and conducted "in the light" but that the motivations of nations (and especially the United States) were to be stewardship in the service of the common good of humanity and "a willingness to forego self-interest in order to promote . . . the happiness . . . of others.[37] This is nothing short of an attempt to collapse the tension between the Sermon on the Mount and the requirements of the political art (described in this book's first chapter) by transforming the latter into the former and by reducing politics and political leadership to nothing more than the business of forming vast, "moral" alliances to expedite the realization of "providential purposes" in history:

> I have seen fools resist Providence before, and I have seen their destruction, as will come upon these again, utter destruction and contempt. That we shall prevail is as sure as that God reigns.[38]

The effect of this Wilsonian legacy on the American perception of the political arts (of moderate reconciliation of differences) is, of course, negative; it reinforces a romantic tendency inherent since colonial America; and it leads to their rejection:

> Policies which seek to maintain a balance of power in world politics, or . . . to preserve our national interests . . . have to be promoted in an idealist framework in order to avoid the rebuke that we are . . . untrue to American tradition. Lastly, the failure of the symbolism of such policies leads to . . . the search for the non-politician, the outsider . . . to lead the national life. He in turn will reassert the idealism of the "true" American tradition. . . . *And the cycle of ideological rejection of political reality begins anew.*[39]

Overall Assessment of Wilson's Statesmanship and Its Consequences

Woodrow Wilson was a high-minded individual, and whatever his blindnesses about the structure of political and other reality, his achievements merit evaluation by high standards. Whatever his ultimate aims, Wilson's primary domestic political endeavor appears to have been the attempt to check and reverse the economic and political influence of a swollen corporate oligarchy in the interest of preserving a meaningful realm of individual moral and economic choice for large numbers of his fellow citizens. Wilson accomplished much of this by throwing in with and helping to propagate an ethic of the common or average man, who required a "common man of uncommon ability," such as Wilson himself, to unify and lead the country in its "providential mission" to redeem the world within actual history. As we have seen, part of this project entailed cultivation of a pedagogic and popular rhetoric aimed at "unlearning" deference to the constitution and to social and economic elites (who were implied to have gained their status solely through fortune or luck). Against thoughtful observers of modern democracy such as Tocqueville, Mill, and Nietzsche, Wilson (like Marx) was convinced that he could engineer an egalitarian society which elevated the rights of the species over the responsibility of the individual to claim them while simultaneously preserving "an infinite individual variety."

The question for our analysis is whether Wilson went farther than was necessary in gaining support for widespread political opposition to established corporate interests inimical to the balance of the American polity. Could Wilson have been elected to presidential office without invoking such extreme egalitarian and redemptive themes in support of the substitution of mighty moral exertion for "mere politics"? Did not Teddy Roosevelt also have some "progressive" aims (less the politically imbalanced oratory of redemption and ubiquitous compassion) and might not these have been sufficient to check undue corporate influence in state legislatures and the national senate?

These questions are difficult to answer demonstratively. My own view is that Wilson went too far in his egalitarian aims because he assumed a fundamental transformation of human nature that would make egalitarianism and "individual variety" compatible and because he thought the idealistic side of America's inheritance could absorb and synthesize its *federalist* inheritance for preserving political stability. But let us for the moment assume that Wilson's political judgment was right about one thing in particular—that sufficient support for the bulk of the progressive program to check the influence of a plutocratic elite would not have been possible without invocation of Wilson's visionary egalitarian and redemptive themes.[40]

If this was, in fact, the case, then the events of the Wilsonian era become more a reflection of the bulk of the American people at the time than of Wilson, their leader. We have in this light the spectacle of a people led in a massive redemptive mission against a plutocracy ensconced in power (as Lincoln prophesied[41]) as the result of another reedemptive mission (a civil war) to enact in history the force of the universal and self-evident truths of the Declaration of Independence; the spectacle of a people with little hope for a moderate escape from the pendulum swings between the two poles of a colonial inheritance bequeathed them by (anti-social) spiritualists on the one hand and (antisocial) adventurers, on the other. (Widespread nihilism may, in time, provide an escape from this cycle, yet such a development may hardly be called "moderate.")

However, if politics must take its bearings from the givens of the moment and if Wilson correctly read what the success of the economic reform movement required, then he simply did what was necessary. If, however, Wilson was wrong and sufficient economic reform to preserve the balance of the republic could have been achieved under the programs of a leader such as Theodore Roosevelt, then Wilson's redemptive egalitarianism simply made conditions more inimical for the sovereignty of individual choice and the very religion that he openly loved, which defended that individual choice on moral grounds. In either case, the task of "creative statesmanship" in the United States now (if these very Wilsonian values are to survive) is surely to move the country away from the simplistic paternalism implicit in the outlook and rhetoric of Wilson and Franklin D. Roosevelt and toward a self-reliance capable of articulating its own purposes within a politics of civility, the formalism of which is more congenial to the life of genuine individual diversity as well as genuine religious faith.[42]

As for the general lessons concerning the art of statesmanship in Wilson's achievements, I have noted and discussed three. To review, the first is the concrete illustration of the power of oratory (in whatever form, including academic journalese) to bring about political change; the second and related lesson involves the particular passions and emotions (and their dangers) invoked by that oratory necessary to move a political system in a more democratic direction; and the third involves the dangers and costs for the arts of statesmanship and politics in millennialist projects.

5

Winston Churchill

THE CAREER OF WINSTON CHURCHILL, SPANNING OVER FIFTY YEARS of public service to his country, is useful in supplying virtual "text-book" illustrations of the characteristics of statesmanship derived from Plato, Aristotle, and Cicero, laid out in this book's first chapter. I wish to employ aspects of Churchill's widely varied public career[1] to give concrete illustrations of the following: 1) the Platonic and Aristotelian idea that the art of the statesman is an architectonic one that orders the other arts and activities; 2) the especially Ciceronian understanding of the vital role of oratory in the statesman's enterprise to order activities and resources in support of the general or public good; and 3) the particular relationship of political leadership to war and the arts of strategy, operations, and tactics. Finally I wish to contrast Churchill's approach to the various problems facing Britain and the world in the twentieth century—an approach strongly influenced by *moral* considerations in support of moderation—with the millennialist outlook of Wilson (and to a lesser degree his disciple, Franklin D. Roosevelt), for the light such an analysis may shed on future prospects for the practice of statesmanship.

The first two considerations—politics as the comprehensive art and oratory or persuasive utterance as its primary vehicle—may be taken in conjunction in Churchill's case, because he explicitly linked them in his own mind (as well as in his words and deeds). In an unpublished article written at the age of twenty-three, Churchill challenged the view that the forces of modern life had relegated the "power of the personality to a thing of the past," for the power of oratory to embody the passions of the multitude was as real now as ever:

He who enjoys it wields a power more durable than that of a great king. He is an independent force in the world. Abandoned by his party . . . stripped of his offices, whoever can command this power is still formidable. . . . [because of] the passions of the multitude . . . [but] Before he can move their tears, his own must flow. To convince them, he must himself believe.[2]

Against the trends of modern specialization, Churchill was apparently implying that the capacity to grasp the idea of the good of the whole country was still necessary and vital and could find its vital power in the passions and commonsense understandings of the "multitudes" if these were properly mobilized and channeled. Certainly this was the principle upon which Churchill acted throughout his life, linking moral, political, geopolitical, and economic considerations in broad, commonsensical perspectives, and going to the public for support. The breadth and lucid competence of Churchill's perspective—political in the Aristotelian sense, oratorical in the Ciceronian—can be concretely illustrated by looking at his narrative and analysis in the first volume of his history of the Second World War, *The Gathering Storm* (1948).

In the first half of this book, Churchill attempts to show that if ever a war could have been prevented (by statesmanship rather than accelerated human evolution), it was the Second World War. He even provides a theme: "How the English-Speaking Peoples Through Their Unwisdom, Carelessness, and Good Nature, Allowed the Wicked to Rearm."[3] The narrative, which is also an analysis, is a logical amalgam of considerations—moral, political, economic, military, social, historical—now thought in much of the academic world to be too specialized for uniting coherently in a single view.

In brief here is Churchill's acount of the critical events and contradictions over two decades that led to the reemergence of Germany as a major military power bent on expansion and hence to the Second World War. The purpose of the narrative, in Churchill's words, is

> to show how easily the tragedy of the Second World War could have been prevented; how the malice of the wicked was reinforced by the weakness of the virtuous; how the structure and habits of democratic states, unless they are welded into larger organisms, lack . . . elements of persistence and conviction. . . .
>
> It was a simple policy to keep Germany disarmed and the victors adequately armed for thirty years, and . . . in the meanwhile . . . build ever more strongly a true League of Nations capable of making sure

treaties were kept. . . . But this modest requirement . . . the victors were unable to supply. They lived from . . . day to day, and from one election to another.[4]

In addition to these "structural" difficulties of democracies in foreign affairs, Churchill cites the *intersection* of the following policies and developments as constituting the conditions that led to the war. First, the French demand (after a century of invasion and the loss of a million and one half men from 1914 to 1918) that Germany's western border be the Rhine River—as a natural barrier to further invasions—was rejected as inconsistent with Wilsonian princples as embodied in the Fourteen Points:

> the Treaty of Versailles left Germany practically intact. She still remained the largest homogeneous racial block in Europe. When Marshall Foch heard of the signing of the Peace Treaty of Versailles he observed with singular accuracy: "This is not Peace. It is an Armistice for twenty years."[5]

Second Churchill observes that the economic clauses of the Treaty "were malignant and silly to an extent that made them obviously futile."[6] The anger of the victors led to huge German reparation requirements, which could never be paid in full, and to German economic stagnation and greater German resentment; and were only able to be met in part through profuse American lending to Germany:

> during the three year 1926 to 1929 the United States was receiving back in the form of debt-instalment indemnities from all quarters about one-fifth of the money which she was lending to Germany with no chance of repayment. . . . History will characterize all these transactions as insane. They helped to breed both the martial curse and the "economic blizzard."[7]

Moreover Churchill observes the British attempted to break this cycle in the Balfour Note, declaring "that Great Britain would collect no more from her debtors, Ally or former enemy, than the United States collected from her." This was rejected by President Coolidge with the quip, "They hired the money, didn't they," followed by increasing U.S. tariffs, making it even more difficult to raise the surplus to pay the British debt to the United States. The first result, says Churchill, "was that everyone put the screw on Germany," leading, in time, to the loss of Germany's working capital, the growth of mushroom trusts, massive inflation, and the elimination of the savings of most of the German middle class.[8]

Third (in Churchill's account), the United States rejected the League of Nations and turned isolationist, while insisting on abstract principles of international practice which served to weaken actual constraints on the rise of Japan and the rearmament of Germany. For example, at the 1921 Washington Conference, broad proposals for disarmament were made by the United States "in odd logic that it would be immoral to disarm the vanquished unless the victors also stripped themselves of their weapons."[9] (Churchill's commonsense maxim throughout the decades leading up to the Second World War was that "the redress of the grievances of the vanquished should precede the disarmament of the victors."[10]) The United States also made it clear that Britain's alliance with Japan would have to end (in the interest of good Anglo-American relations), with the resulting alienation of Japan from any Western ties: "Many links were sundered which might afterwards have proved of decisive value to peace."[11] And, in another example of the application of Wilsonian principles (prior to its turn inward), the United States insisted on the breakup of the Austro-Hungarian Empire, leading, in Churchill's view, to the "Balkanization of Southeastern Europe" and "the consequent relative aggrandizement of Prussia and the German Reich."[12] In brief the United States, France, and Britain concentrated on getting their debt payments and reparations (also financed by U.S. loans) and ignored the signs of secret (and increasingly open) German rearmament.[13] Still, Churchill notes, if the political will had been present, the war could have been prevented without much sacrifice prior to the consolidation of Hitler's power: "Up until 1934 at least German rearmament could have been prevented without the loss of a single life. It was not time that was lacking."[14]

My general points in making this excursion into Churchill's account of the causes of the Second World War (which, like Foch, he believed to be merely a continuation of the war of 1914–18) have been to illustrate the comprehensiveness of Churchill's perspective and to illustrate the power (and his belief in the power) of good political rhetoric.

On this first point, it is clear that Churchill's perspective (in these examples and countless others) was consistently statesmanlike and directed toward the general good, not so much from subjective intentions, as from the comprehensiveness of his out-look, which sought for the practical causes of events across the various "compartments" of modern civilization and linked what-ever variety of considerations—moral, economic, military, etc.—was necessary to explain events with a view to taking practical action for their remedy. The consistency of Churchill's perspective will become apparent to anyone who begins to read his works and speeches. Yet it can also be employed to explain why he was so often censured and criticized by those required to take a narrower view by either their official positions or more limited capacities. For example the Dardanelles campaign and the losses at Gallipoli during the First World War were widely held at the time to be the failure of Churchill as first lord of the Admiralty, for going against the better judgment of his admirals on technical naval questions. (The events in question led to Churchill's resignation from the cabinet.) But the records now available show that the issue was, in fact, one of political or strategic judgment about where Britain's resources should be committed in order to break up the deadly stalemate on the Western front.[15] If Churchill was guilty of an offense in this case, it was of thinking as prime minis-ter while he was merely in charge of the navy; that is, of holding to a scope of vision that he did not have the authority to imple-ment. When his scope of vision and actual authority finally coin-cided during the Second World War, he benefited his country immeasurably.

The second point in these illustrations from *The Gathering Storm* concerns Churchill's view of oratory, which appears very similar to that of Cicero's character Crassus. (That is, the purpose of Churchill's book is didactic and rhetorical—the writing of history was for him primarily a branch of morals.[16]) In this particular regard, Churchill appears more "Roman" than "Greek," dis-daining theoretical inquiry into practical affairs for its own sake and concentrating instead on the force of persuasive utterance (whether written or spoken) to bring about practical change. Here are some of Churchill's own words on the subject as a young man in a letter to his mother, describing what his called his one "mental flaw": "I do not care so much for the principles I advocate as for the impression which my words produce & the reputation they give me."[17] (Cicero, of course, would have said this was not a "flaw" at all, provided the reputation desired was for public service, as it was in Churchill's case.) And, on the issue of "theory and practice," here is Churchill explicitly: "A man's life must be nailed to a cross of either Thought or Action."[18] Churchill's life was indeed nailed to a cross of political action but not in any narrow party or partisan sense (another reason he was so often criticized). Rather his was a life dedicated to political action in support of what was good for the British people: action made vital through good political oratory, for example, through the power of informed and well-crafted speech and writing to influence independent minds.

Another aspect of statesmanship, which Churchill's career supplies ample illustration for, concerns its relationship to the arts of strategy and war. As we saw earlier, Plato's Stranger required the statesman to know only enough of the art of strategy to be able to say when to call it into play and when to turn initiative over to strategists or generals. But this is vague advice, because it does not take up the issue of whether and when the statesman is to enter into the details of at least general military planning. (Some of the dangers of the strict isolation of military from political planning can be seen in the German experience during the before and during the First World War, when Chancellor Bethmann-Hollweg was excluded from knowledge of even the general strategy for the invasion of France.[19]) More explicit guidance on this subject can be found at the level of general principle in the admonition of von Clausewitz, philosopher of war, that both military strategy and tactics should take their bearings from the *political* objective in question and vary as it varies, if confusion and wasted effort are not to reign.[20] As Professor McPherson has shown in his lucid chapter on Lincoln's strategy in the Civil War,[21] this was a principle that Lincoln grasped well, altering both northern military strategy and tactics as the political aim of the war evolved from that of suppressing a rebellion to the total emancipation of all slaves.

There is no doubt that Churchill also grasped this general (Clausewitzean) principle. He viewed every military engagement from the standpoint of its likely consequences for the future of British influence (and British principles of justice);[22] he was fond of saying that at the highest levels, politics and strategy were one;[23] and he was, to cite an illustration, largely responsible for the direction of Allied operations in 1942–43, especially the campaigns in North Africa, Sicily, and Italy.[24] (Churchill was also fond of the

American expression, "overall strategic concept"—in spite of its awkwardness—and made it a theme of his "iron curtain" speech at Fulton, Missouri, in 1946.) In addition to engaging competently in grand strategy,[25] Churchill (like Lincoln before he found Grant) intervened in the details of military operations both as first lord of the Admiralty in the First World War and as prime minister during the second.[26] An interesting question for our inquiry is whether this Churchillian practice constituted good statesmanship.

The short answer here is that it is probably not possible to come to a general conclusion other than "it depends." Churchill was fascinated by war from an early age (for the complexity of its challenges) and had seen intense combat as a junior officer in several nineteenth-century "colonial wars," inflicting casualties at close quarters himself.[27] His intense interest in war and war planning caused his mind and energies to focus in its presence and resulted in significant contributions to his country which perhaps no other individual could have made. His readying of the British navy between 1911 and 1914, his supervision of the channel ports defense in 1914–15, his personal involvement in the crucial six-day defense of Antwerp in 1914, and his early efforts to develop British tank and air warfare capabilities come to mind in this regard.[28] Yet there were other instances where the degree of Churchill's involvement in the details of strategy, operations, and tactics may be seen as grounds for censure. (I do not have in mind here the failure of the Dardanelles campaign, which the record clearly shows was a matter of widespread responsibility at civilian and military levels.[29]) On this score Gordon Craig cites, for instance, the consequences of Churchill's decisions to aid Greece in March 1941 and to elevate pursuit of Rommel in Egypt to high priorities, as instrumental in the fall of Singapore, and, in turn, advancement of the "dissolution of the British Empire over which Churchill had vowed he would not preside."[30] (Craig's remarks are made with the benefit of hindsight—at the time General de Gaulle also emphasized the importance of the North African campaign.[31]) Doubtless Churchill's intense interest in warfare led him to intervene in details of planning and execution which another leader would have shunned, but his ability to function so focused and energetically under crisis conditions also made him a very effective leader of his country during war, combining skills of strategic judgment, diplomacy (especially vis-à-vis Franklin D.

Roosevelt), and oratory to advance British interests beyond what the British commonwealth's material strengths would have seemed likely to achieve.

If there is a general conclusion about the relationship of statesmanship to the conduct of war in the case of Churchill, it would seem to be that the question about the degree of the stateman's involvement in details of operations is a matter of indifference at the level of principle and depends on the individual leader in question. What is essential, however, for statesmanlike leadership during wartime—as the cases of both Churchill and Lincoln show—is the capacity to grasp and give effect to two related ideas: that the military means must vary as the political object of the war varies and that harmony must be preserved (as Clausewitz observed) among the triad of political leadership, military leadership, and public opinion or "the passions of the people." At this level Churchill performed superbly.

The third general aspect of Churchill's achievements as political leader I wish to inspect involves their relationship to, and contrast with, the millennialist outlook described in the preceding chapter on Woodrow Wilson. Churchill is especially interesting for the contrast he provides to Wilson, Franklin Roosevelt, and American millennialism, because Churchill (like Wilson) tended to approach problems from a *moral* standpoint rather than an expressly political one (except when political is understood in its broadest sense). Let us first try to establish this point. Martin Gilbert has summarized Churchill's "political philosophy" as it evolved over a lifetime:

> Churchill's political philosophy was supremely simple in concept; it was based on the preservation and protection of individual freedom and a decent way of life, if necessary, by means of State aid and power; on the protection of the individual against the misuse of State power; on the pursuit of political compromise and the middle way in order both to maintain and to improve the existing framework of Parliamentary democracy; on the protection of small States against the aggression of more powerful States; and on the linking together of all democratic States to protect themselves from the curse and calamity of war.[32]

In my view Gilbert is correct about the simplicity of Churchill's outlook. In essence his approach throughout a lifetime was to

throw all of his very abundant energy into causes and reforms in
support of independence of individual judgment and minimal
standards of decency for all. As he told a friend: "As long as I
am fighting a cause, I am not afraid of anything. Nor do I weary
as the struggle proceeds."[33] And, on the same general point in a
letter to his son in 1931: "It is a great comfort when one minds
the questions one cares about far more than office or Party or
friendships."[34] Indeed for a "politician," Churchill was singularly
inattentive to calculations of public feeling or party loyalty,
changing party affiliations *twice* in one political lifetime. Here are
some of his reflections on party affiliation and political
consistency:

> There is an England which stretches far beyond the well-drilled
> masses who are assembled by party machinery . . . an England of wise
> men who gaze without self-deception at the failings and follies of
> both political parties. . . . of "poor men" who increasingly doubt the
> sincerity of party philanthropy.[35]

> A statesman in contact with the moving current of events and anxious
> to keep the ship on an even keel and steer a steady course may lean
> all his weight now on one side and now on the other. His arguments
> in each case when contrasted can be shown to be . . . contradictory in
> spirit and opposite in direction. . . . *We cannot call this inconsistency.* The
> only way a man can remain consistent amid changing circumstances
> is to change with them *while pursuing the same dominating purpose.*[36]

On the issues of reform and fundamental standards of decency,
Churchill was also a pioneer in England. It was he, in a speech in
1906, who coined the idea of a safety net below which we would
not permit anyone to fall:

> I do not want to impair the vigour of competition, but we can do
> much to mitigate the consequences of failure. We want to draw a line
> below which we will not allow persons to live and labour, yet above
> which they may compete with all the strength of their manhood. We
> do not want to pull down the structure of science and civilization—
> but to spread a net over the abyss.[37]

Nor did Churchill's concern stop at speeches. During the latter
half of the first decade of the twentieth century, Churchill, as a
liberal cabinet minister, was instrumental in the passage of a series
of legislative acts that provided for labor arbitration procedures,

restraints on employers' prerogatives, the beginnings of compulsory unemployment insurance, prison reform, compulsory public education, and progressive taxation policies.[38] Gilbert says in summary of Churchill's reform efforts:

> Churchill's ideas, speeches and legislative work between 1908 and 1910 helped to launch a revolution in the social philosophy of Britain; a bloodless revolution of substantial reform inside the existing social structures. As such it was his aim to reform what was bad and to preserve what was good in society, by evolution and fair dealing.
> Churchill never abandoned his philosophy of the middle course.[39]

My general point in these examples is that many of Churchill's aims coincided with the aims of American progressives, but his arguments for these various measures were generally commonsensical and moderate rather than millennialist. In contrast to the rhetoric of Woodrow Wilson, there is in Churchill's political rhetoric no hint of a providential plan for the progressive reshaping of social reality[40] nor any pandering to the "wisdom" of the working classes (or on the subject of the need for compassion toward them). Instead we find only forceful, persuasive, commonsensical arguments about fundamental decency and the need for change:

> Neither pity nor charity can inspire the Acts of a Government. The interest of the community alone must direct them.[41]

> No one is to be pitied for having to work hard, for nature has contrived a special reward for the man who works hard. It gives him an extra relish, which enables him to gather in a brief space from simple pleasures a satisfaction in search of which the social idler wanders vainly. . . . But this reward . . . is snatched away from the man who won it, if the hours of labour be too severe to leave him any time to enjoy what he has won.[42]

> I think it is our duty to use the strength and the resources of the State to arrest the ghastly waste not merely of human happiness but of national health and strength which follows when a working man's home which has taken him years to get together is broken up through a long spell of unemployment.[43]

> We have against us all the modern money power. . . . We are resolved if we can to prevent any class from steadily absorbing under the shelter of law the wealth in creation of which they have borne no share,

wealth which belongs not to them, but to the community, wealth which they can only secure by obstructions, far more injurious and wasteful than can be measured by their immediate gains.[44]

Similarly, in contrast to the unrealistic (and even utopian in some cases) hopes of the supporters of disarmament in the face of German rearmament in the 1930s, Churchill's views and arguments remained realistic and commonsensical, anticipating no major change in human nature. Against the views of the radical left about an imminent "new world order" based on socialism and pacifism[45] and against those others who first demanded punitive reparations and within a decade did a volte-face and supported outright German appeasement and a revision of the Versailles Treaty, Churchill articulated a coherent, practical course of action from 1918 on. He saw the problem facing Britain as the preservation of individual freedom and parliamentary democracy in the face of the rise of Bolshevism on the left and (in time) the rise of fascism on the right. Churchill thought that moral forces must be adhered to in foreign affairs[46] and that here was a case where "Right may walk hand in hand with Might," where moral idealism and strategic prudence coincided.[47]

As Churchill repeatedly stated, the solution to preventing another war was to redress the justified German grievances early, while the Entente powers were still armed and strong, to prevent any future alliance between an extremist Germany and the Soviet Union, and certainly not to accelerate western disarmament in the face of a growing German rearmament and territorial expansion (in the fantastic hope of an accelerated transformation of human nature). Here is Martin Gilbert's summary of Churchill's comprehensive outlook, which coherently combined both international and domestic considerations as early as 1921:

> Here then were the three interwoven strands of Churchill's political philosophy: "the appeasement of class bitterness" at home, "the appeasement of fearful hatreds and antagonisms abroad," and the defense of Parliamentary democracy and democratic values in Britain, in Western Europe, and in the territories under British rule or control. Whenever possible, the method to be used was conciliation . . . the path of moderation. . . . but in the last resort it might be necessary to defend those values by force of arms.[48]

Churchill's views on foreign policy and foreign obligations can be drawn out further by contrasting them with the more millennialist outlook of Wilsonian internationalism and Rooseveltian "Americanism," both of which (as variations on Gladstonian Liberalism[49]) assumed a basic transformation in universal human nature as the basis of "progress." Churchill, by contrast, did not think that the movement of civilization was from self-interest to increasing altruism but rather (like Aristotle[50]) involved the differentiation and refinement of self-interest toward higher (i.e., more noble and rational) forms. As one author insightfully observes on this point:

> The ascent from barbarism to full civilization does not, in Churchill's view, entail a movement from the depths of narrow self-seeking to the peaks of selfless altruism. As one becomes more civilized his concern does not shift from a regard for his own good to a self-denying desire to benefit others. . . . A proper view of moral obligation for individuals and for nations lay, in Churchill's view, closer to the extreme of calculation in one's own interest than to the extreme of self-denying duty to benefit others.[51]

> Churchill distinguished his understanding of the political nature of human excellence from the Socialist's view . . . and from the view . . . promoted by the mass democratic regime which emerged . . . after World War I. *In its tendency to separate the social from the political, its depreciation of politics and elevation of economics and its opposition to political leadership led Churchill to suggest that a modern mass democracy had lost sight of the fact that man is a political animal.*[52]

It is this basic difference about the *enduring* role of politics and statesmanship in providing for the *fullest* human possibilities that sets Churchill's views off from those of Wilson and Roosevelt, more so than simple differences over Britain's preferential trade agreements with members of its Empire. For the vision of even a pragmatist like Roosevelt was ultimately grounded in, and directed by, a hope for the progressive elimination of the very political role that Roosevelt was himself performing, as testified to by the compiler of the entire Roosevelt-Churchill wartime correspondence:

> Franklin Roosevelt . . . tutored by Woodrow Wilson . . . possessed a calm, quite conviction that Americanism was so very sensible . . . that societies would adopt those values and systems if only given the chance. It was the city-on-a-hill-an-example-for-all-the-world-to-follow approach that FDR preferred. . . . The final goal was progression to-

ward a homogeneous world—however unlikely full achievement be. *John Winthrop and the Puritans would have been proud.*[53]

It had been Europe which forced the collapse of Wilson's dream, at home and abroad, and FDR had no intention of letting that happen again.[54]

In my view this difference between Churchill on the one hand and Wilson-Roosevelt on the other, over the relative importance of politics and statesmanship as a permanent feature of the best human possibilities, is illustrative of the central issue in the political and ideological disputes of our century. It is a theme we shall return to in the concluding chapter of this book.

OVERALL ASSESSMENT OF CHURCHILL'S STATESMANSHIP

I have tried to show (as have others) that Churchill's consistent political focus (never falling below what he called "the level of events") and accomplished oratory are unambiguous illustrations of the successful application of the ancient ideal of statesmanship in the (relatively) modern world and within a liberal-individualist context. In addition Churchill's rather unique abilities under crisis conditions were responsible for decisive contributions to his country's welfare, which, arguably, no other individual could have provided, for example, his readying of the British navy from 1911 to 1914, his defense of Antwerp in 1914, and his political leadership and strategic judgment during the battle of Britain in 1940.

Yet it is certain *ideas* of this thoughtful and literate man of action, as found in his speeches and books, which are perhaps his greatest legacy to the art of statesmanship within the modern Liberal tradition. Like George Washington (and unlike many theoretical writers), Churchill thought that belief in the importance of individual liberty and individual judgment could be coherently combined with belief in the importance of political obligation to do great things—that individualism and civic virtue were not incompatible. And he provides, as we have seen in his various policies and their rationales, concrete illustrations of how these two general perspectives may be intelligently combined. Second Churchill's view of the relative (importance and) unimportance of party affiliation, and his success in achieving programs in spite of his elevation of moral principle over party loyalties, shows that a statesmanlike focus on the general good can have effect in the modern world. And third Churchill's common sense and articulate defenses of many domestic and international reforms provide an example and an antidote for the excesses of millennialist rationales and justifications, which are still respectful of the continued importance of the arts of politics and statesmanship in making public life better. If there was an aspect of Churchill's style that we might characterize as unstatesmanlike, and not to be emulated, it was his outspokenness and occasional lack of prudence in public concerning those with whom he differed, a trait perhaps deriving from a strong personal need always to be actively engaged in a cause or conflict.[55]

6

Charles de Gaulle

As in the case of Churchill, the life and career of Charles de Gaulle provide virtual textbook illustrations of the application of the art of statesmanship in the (relatively) modern world. There are six aspects we shall explore for the light shed on our general subject and on de Gaulle's own achievements as leader of the French nation during the Second World War and after 1958. The first is de Gaulle's explicit belief in and use of good political rhetoric (in books, articles, and speeches) to give practical force to ideas, educate fellow-citizens, and *unify* an historically divided people. Second is the matter of de Gaulle's general perspective, which was consistently statesmanlike in focus and had much to do (as in the cases of Washington and Churchill) with his practical success. The third aspect involves the qualities necessary to effect an explicit constitutional refounding of his country (the Fifth Republic). Fourth is de Gaulle's understanding of the importance of military force in the genesis and perpetuation of political and governmental authority, as well as the necessity for its subordination to political authority. The fifth aspect involves de Gaulle's (very Rousseauan) attitudes toward political parties and parliamentary tactics and their relationship to the common or general good and to the state's authority; and toward transnational associations and their relationships to the authority of states and the welfare of various peoples. The final aspect of de Gaulle's statesmanship to inspect involves this devout French Catholic's views of "history" and destiny, none of which evince any millennialist belief in the feasibility or desirability of a fundamental transformation of political reality.

Charles de Gaulle, as his most recent biographer explicitly states, was an orator.[1] He relied heavily on the force of well-crafted and informed *words* to influence his fellow citizens and move them in the direction he thought France should go. His initial rhetorical efforts take the form of lectures, articles, and books addressed primarily to fellow officers on the directions the French army should take to dissuade or defeat another German invasion, in particular the necessity for development of armored units, manned by professional forces, and capable of aggressive maneuver.[2] (De Gaulle was an opponent of Petain's passive, "Maginot line" mentality.) Frustrated by opposition within the army and alarmed by German rearmament in the 1930s, de Gaulle turned his persuasive efforts toward politicians and, as he says, "public opinion," in hopes of gaining support there. In his BBC broadcasts from London after the "fall of France" on 18 and 19 June 1940, de Gaulle relied on the force of his words and personality (and the support of Winston Churchill) to revivify French political authority and military resistance. During the war, facing opposition from Roosevelt, the Vichy government, and later, Churchill, and with little material support, de Gaulle relied primarily upon the effect of speeches and pronouncements to articulate the French view of international matters in what would be the postwar world.[3] (De Gaulle was convinced early on that the Allies would be victorious.[4]) In 1945 and 1946 de Gaulle relied (unsuccessfully at the time) on spéeches to the French people for support of a new constitution which would overcome the divisiveness of the old "regime of parties" and provide for a new, invigorated executive capable of providing a stable and authoritative framework for the daily business of the nation. During his tenure as president of the Fifth Republic (from 1958 to 1969), de Gaulle used forceful, carefully orchestrated press conferences to explain his policies and preserve his mystique as a leader.[5] After his service as wartime leader and then after his resignation as president in 1969, de Gaulle relied on the use of published memoirs to explain his various decisions to the public and provide documentation for historians to study.

In brief there be no doubt of de Gaulle's belief in, and demonstration of, the power of words delivered in a public space to effect political change or shore-up and preserve political authority (de Gaulle had a strong Rousseauan belief in legitimacy deriving from the "general will"[6]), by touching or "turning around" forces deep within the human personality. As his lifelong associate and friend, André Malraux, makes clearer than any other writer, politics for de Gaulle was still an art of the soul[7] and could no longer exist once all public business was reduced to simply the assurance and distribution of economic benefits. (Insofar as the Fifth Republic finally resembled such a situation, de Gaulle's pessimism about "the end of Western civilization"—of which more later—is perhaps understandable.[8])

Before leaving the subject of de Gaulle's oratory or political rhetoric, let us note its characteristics. De Gaulle's speeches and books are characterized by their simplicity of expression, their directness, and their emphasis on historical symbols capable of unifying those divided by more immediate concerns behind the memory of the greatness and continuity of French civilization. On de Gaulle's style, Malraux notes:

> I knew that this book, heir to the *Memoires de guerre,* would be a Roman simplification of events—the simplification by which, in literature as in architecture, Rome imposes its domination so strongly. . . . He was not Latin; he was Roman, which means almost the opposite.[9]

Perhaps we should allow de Gaulle to illustrate these points for himself. A good instance of "Gaullist rhetoric" is to be found in his two broadcasts from London on 18 and 19 June 1940, when he had virtually nothing to offer for the service of his nation but the power of his words and personality:

> Frenchmen must now be fully aware that all ordinary forms of authority have disappeared.
>
> Faced by the bewilderment of my countrymen, by the disintegration of a government in thrall to the enemy, by the fact that the institutions of my country are incapable, at the moment, of functioning, I, General de Gaulle, a French soldier and military leader, realize that I speak for France.
>
> In the name of France, I make the following solemn declaration:
>
> It is the bounden duty of all Frenchmen who still bear arms to continue the struggle. For them to lay down their arms, to evacuate any position of military importance, or to hand over any part of French territory. . . . would be a crime against our country. . . .
>
> Whatever happens, the flame of French resistance must not and shall not die.[10]

The pedagogic side of de Gaulle's rhetoric will become apparent in excerpts from various speeches and works adduced in illustration of other aspects of his statesmanship. Here I simply note insightful testimony on this score from Henry Kissinger in his 1965 book, *The Troubled Partnership:*

> He judges the merit of a policy not only by technical criteria but also by its contribution to France's sense of identity. His deeper objective is pedagogical: to teach his people and perhaps his continent attitudes of independence and self-reliance. Consequently the dispute between France and the United States centers, in part, around the philosophical issue of how nations cooperate.[11]

Kissinger's observation about de Gaulle's capacity to blend the technical and the pedagogic points us toward the second aspect of de Gaulle's statesmanship I wish to consider—the consistent focus of de Gaulle's perspective, which was *political* in the Aristotelian sense of politics as the architectonic art. Here is Malraux's description of de Gaulle's general perspective:

> Attempts have been made to describe him through psychology. Where he is concerned such attempts seem vain to me. . . . *his intelligence had more to do with the level of his thought* (what Chateaubriand called the intelligence of greatness of spirit) more than the thought itself or from insight, although he had these.[12]

And on the issue of his temporal orientation, here is biographer Jean Lacouture:

> he played every stroke with the medium or long term in view—farther ahead, at all events, than any of his partners (with the possible exception of the Communists). This notion . . . is still clearer in this observation of René Massigli . . . "de Gaulle can see over and beyond the horizon."[13]

My point here is that de Gaulle's focus was always on what was good for France, as a whole and over the long haul, and this led him to link together whatever considerations were relevant to the problem at hand—political, military, economic, psychological, and so on. This is clear even in de Gaulle's early writings as an army officer. Here is an illustration from *Le Fil D'Epée* (1931), a book written by Major de Gaulle to encourage a new "spirit of enterprise" in the French army, which moves on to suggest the need for a new system of professional education to nurture greater mutual understanding between political and military leaders:

The statesman and the soldier bring . . . to a common task very different characters, methods, and anxieties. The former reaches his goal
by roundabout ways, the latter by direct approach. The one is long-
sighted though his vision may be clouded, sees realities as complex. . . .
The other with clear eyes sees what there is to be seen straight in
front of his nose and thinks it simple and capable of being controlled
by resolution.[14]

One would think that an enlightened State would see the wisdom
of training a political, administrative, and military elite, by means of
studies undertaken in common, so that there might be a body of men,
competent in all three departments to direct the nation in time of
war . . . it would also have the advantage of clarifying, in times of
peace, the duties and legal standing of the armed forces of the
nation.[15]

My aim in selecting these quotations is to show that their perspective is that of the highest level of political leadership, that is,
the perspective of what was best for France as a whole in dealing
with the problem of its defense against another German armed
invasion. When the problems facing his country changed, de
Gaulle shifted his attention but never his span, which remained
statesmanlike, that is comprehensive enough to link the "technical" and the "moral" considerations at hand. (De Gaulle even
wrote in *Le Fil D'Epée* that the military problem was essentially a
moral one.)

Consider in this context de Gaulle's lucidly stated views on economic matters as president of the Fifth Republic, a subject where
neither his genius nor interests really lay.[16]

What guidance must I give the economic effort so that it should measure up to the policies to which I was about to commit France? From
the beginning I felt that it was simply a matter of common sense. The
country could only thrive internally and carry weight abroad if its
activity was in tune with the age. In an industrial era, it must be
industrial . . . it must be competitive . . . it must cultivate research . . .
it must undergo a profound transformation.[17]

at my level, I was concerned with the Plan,[18] because it was all-
embracing, because it fixed the targets, established a hierarchy of
necessities and priorities . . . and because it compensated for the drawbacks of freedom without sacrificing its advantages.[19]

I was concerned with international competition for this was the lever
which could activate our business world . . . hence my determination

to promote the Common Market ... I was concerned with invest-
ments ... to modernize our equipment. ... I was concerned with
"advanced" industries. ... I was concerned with the currency. ... I
was therefore to give France a model franc whose parity was to remain
constant as long as I was in power.[20]

Nor were these economic aims idle speculation. Together with
subordinates animated by economic problems (such as Pompi-
dou), de Gaulle moved France into the "industrial era." Here is
the assessment on this score by English historian Paul Johnson in
his history of the twentieth century, *Modern Times*:

Under de Gaulle, in short, France became for the first time a modern,
industrialized country, in the forefront of technical progress. ... It
was the very antithesis of France of the 1930s. *Such a reversal of deep
historical trends is very rare in history, particularly for an old nation. It gives
de Gaulle a claim to be considered the outstanding statesman of modern
times.*[21]

Again my general point in this excursion (into de Gaulle's economic achievements) has been to show the comprehensiveness of
his perspective, which was consistently focused on what was good
for his country. When the most severe problem facing it was military, he turned his attention to that subject; when economic, to
that subject; and when the problem involved the basic structure
of France's political system, de Gaulle turned his attention to that.
(Although I believe the point is obvious, this pattern suggests that
one criterion of statesmanship is the willingness to take on the
major problems facing a body politic rather than simply tend to
peripheral ones.) The last problem listed brings us to our next
subject, de Gaulle's refounding of the French state in 1958 (and
afterward), a refounding necessary for the political stability and
executive power to accomplish the economic achievements just
noted. In spite of Paul Johnson's claim, carefully speaking, it
would seem that the new constitution introduced by de Gaulle
makes up a stronger claim to great statesmanship than the economic and other achievements that it made possible. De Gaulle's
ideas for a new constitution also permit us to take up his view of
political parties—one effect of its elimination of the proportional
representation voting system was to organize four major parties
into two major, less divisive blocs.[22]

De Gaulle's views on what was necessary for good governance

of the French are set out in his famous "Bayeux speech" delivered in 1946. Although he had to wait another twelve years to see them come into effect and endure the spectacle of the French Republic's repetition of the parliamentary squabbles of the Third, the central ideas of the current French constitution (written by the Gaullist, Michel Debré in 1958) are present in the Bayeux speech. Here is some of what de Gaulle said at Bayeux in Normandy, a year after the close or the Second World War. After observing that France's "salvation" during the war had *not* come from the "earlier pattern of government" but from those "who set aside any feelings of party or class," de Gaulle goes on to analyze the problems facing France. He observes, matter of factly and for a variety of reasons (including the "natural Gallic temperament, which is so prone to division and quarrels"[23]), that

> the rivalry of parties in our country is a natural characteristic, that of always questioning everything . . . often overshadowing the major interests of the country. . . . it is therefore essential for the future of our country and of democracy that our Constitution show itself aware of this and take care to. . . . retain the cohesion of the Government . . . and authority of the State.[24]

De Gaulle goes on to observe that a major dilemma facing France (and other states in the modern world) is how to achieve the efficiency necessary for its industrial and economic organization and functioning, without succumbing to the promise of order that only dictatorship can provide in the midst of chaos. The answer is "to realize how necessary it is that our new democratic institutions should themselves compensate for the effects of our perpetually ebullient policy."[25] De Gaulle's major proposal is for a much strengthened executive power no longer dependent on a divisive parliament to *secure* the basic context, as it were, within which the dynamism of democracy can occur:

> It is therefore from the head of the state, placed above party feeling . . . that executive power must flow. His should be the task of nominating ministers and . . . of course, the Prime Minister. . . . To him would fall the task of promulgating laws and decrees . . . the task of presiding over the Councils of the Government. . . . On him devolves the duty, if the nation is in danger, of safeguarding national independence.[26]

> Let us be lucid and strong enough both to make for ourselves and to keep rules of national life which will tend to gather us together at a

time when we are driven ceaselessly to division amongst ourselves.
Our whole history is the alteration of the immense sorrows of a divided people, and, the fruitful grandeur of a free nation grouped
under the aegis of a strong state.[27]

A dozen years later, in the midst of a national crisis over the
Algerian question, de Gaulle was able to see this vision given effect
in a new constitution, with himself as the new president. Here is
a recent assessment by political scientist Stanley Hoffmann of de
Gaulle's constitutional achievements (which for a decade were able
to accommodate a socialist president):

> What have been the main contributions of the constitutional system
> to the French political community. The most obvious has been govern-
> mental stability after almost a century of weak cabinets and presidents
> with minimal power. . . . De Gaulle has succeeded, posthumously, in
> his attempt at synthesizing previously incompatible traditions; *in this
> respect, it is he who brought an end to the divisions created by the French
> revolution.* . . . It is impossible to prove that none of this would have
> happened if French parliamentarism had survived . . . but it is diffi-
> cult to believe that a system that led each party to "cultivate its differ-
> ences" (because of proportional representation) and led cabinets to
> immobility (because of coalitions) would have been as equally
> effective.[28]

For our purposes it is sufficient to note that against extraordinary odds (and against Professor Hoffmann's concessions to the
school of "aggregate social forces"), de Gaulle achieved a refounding of his country, which imposed a much needed unity *that the
parliamentary system showed itself (from 1870 to 1958) unable to generate itself,* and was still true to democratic requirements for majoritarian consent. How this was achieved is interesting for the light it
sheds on the qualities of leadership necessary for the refounding
of a people (short of armed revolution). To appreciate de Gaulle's
achievement (as well as his ruthlessness) in this regard, it is in-
structive to look briefly at the conditions that led to his ascension
to power in 1958 during the Algerian crisis. This exploration will
also illustrate Max Weber's claim about the demons of politics and
their incompatibility with the god of love.[29]

The situation in France in 1958 was literally that of a country
on the verge of either civil war or a coup d'état by the French
army based in Algeria. The immediate cause of the crisis was a
Muslim rebellion for independence in Algeria against the more

than one million French *colons* there and the army that protected them. Adding to the intensity of the situation was the resentment of the army over its loss in Indochina (Vietnam) in 1954, which it attributed in part to lack of support from the Fourth Republic's politicians. De Gaulle at this time was still "retired" at his home in Colombey Les Deux Eglises, where he had gone in 1946 to write his war memoirs. Overtures were made to him to save the situation by various politicians who thought he might be able to control the army. On the condition of six-month emergency powers followed by a referendum on a new constitution granting the president much greater powers, de Gaulle took over leadership of France, acting quickly to avert a coup. He handled the army by telling them that he understood them, implying that he would not grant Algerian independence (on some occasions making this explicit[30]) and that he would bring their leader in Algeria, General Salan, to Paris (where he was rendered ineffectual). De Gaulle handled the "politicians" by allowing them to glimpse the threat of violence by the army.[31]

The outcome of all of this was that Algeria was granted independence (with ties to France); no coup d'état occurred; France acquired a new constitution and a new president (by 1962 elected through universal suffrage); and those Algerian Muslims who had cooperated with the French were left to their fate (a horrible slaughter[32]). De Gaulle has been criticized for lying to the army (a secret organization of which made many subsequent, unsuccessful attempts on de Gaulle's life) and for leaving in the lurch with the words, "Eh bien—vous suffrirez,"[33] the quarter million Algerians who had cooperated with the French colonial administration. Still de Gaulle's decisiveness and political acumen in the crisis not only averted a possible military take over in metropolitan France[34] but led to the adoption of a new constitution, which almost all agree has greatly benefited France.

It is difficult to see that any other individual in France at the time could have performed this service, bridging from a military crisis to the preservation (and actual strengthening—in spite of cries of "Bonapartism") of French republican institutions and their heritage. This series of events also highlights the necessity (as do the cases of Washington and Hamilton) in constitutional foundings of having available leaders with military skills and traits, who also understand that military considerations must ultimately be subordinated to political ones for the long-term health and well-being of nations.

De Gaulle's focus on the French *nation*, in a world of nations, is interesting for its contrast with the views of European (and world) transnational integrationists, such as Jean Monnet, de Gaulle's "antagonist" for three decades. It also raises the issue of whether the art of statesmanship can accommodate a perspective intent on eliminating the state as the dominant "unit" of human integration. In de Gaulle's view the state was the authoritative order of the nation, a grouping forged from the deepest human emotions, especially those generated by war. Jean Lacouture suggests that this was precisely why de Gaulle strove so hard to keep France in the Second World War—as a basis for the rebirth of the French nation:

> For General de Gaulle. . . . It was war that shaped nations. . . . However ardently one might wish to avoid it and with whatever reluctance one was drawn into it, war was an essential moment in the great casting of history, the point at which the sculptor's chisel cut into the stone and fashioned what tomorrow was to be the likeness of a nation. Was not Charles de Gaulle the man who first on 18 June, "kept France in the war" because he believed that it was in that terrible furnace that the country would forge its re-birth, winning its right to exist and its dignity as a partner?[35]

Furthermore, given the role of force in human history and the state's monopoly on the means of force, states would remain essential for the protection of national interests. De Gaulle wrote:

> But hope though we may, what reasons have we for thinking that passion and self-interest, the root cause of armed conflict in men and nations will cease to operate . . . that human nature will ever become something other than it is. . . . In whatever direction the world may move, it will never be able to do without the final arbitrament of arms.[36]

> I repeat that . . . there is and can be no Europe other than a Europe of the States—except of course, for myths, fictions, pageants.
> A so-called "integrated Europe," which would have no policy, would come to depend on someone outside, and that someone would have a policy of his own. There would perhaps be a federator, but it would not be a European.[37]

For de Gaulle there should be an allied Europe to provide a "third way" between the super powers, but it was to be a Europe of States *(Europe des Patries)*, along the lines of the European alliances that were formed to defend against Eastern invasions centuries before, bound together by a common culture created by poets and writers, not technocrats.[38] How different were the views of Jean Monnet, the "father of European integration" and of the European Economic Community:

> General de Gaulle's proposals ... are based on notions that are out of date. They forget the lessons of our most recent history ... that it is impossible to solve Europe's problems with States which retain their full national sovereignty.[39]

> It is not a question of solving political problems which, as in the past, divide the forces that seek domination or superiority. It is a question of *inducing civilization to make fresh progress by beginning to change the form of relationship between countries* and applying the principle of equality between peoples and between countries. *People no longer want their future to depend on the skill or ambition of their Governments.* They do not want ephemeral solutions ... they want there to be established in our countries an organization, a procedure, that will make possible collective discussion and decision.[40]

> *The sovereign nations* of the past can no longer solve the problems of the present; *they cannot ensure their own progress or control their own future.* And the (European) Community itself is only a stage on the way to the organized world of tomorrow.[41]

In my view the fundamental philosophical difference between de Gaulle and Monnet (and the respective positions they represent) is this: For de Gaulle, the sovereign state, with its monopoly in legitimacy and armed force, is still the "organization" best able to provide a balance between order and liberty for its members. For Monnet (the father of French economic planning as well), the fundamental problem facing us—as the quotations above make clear—is not first and foremost about the balance between order and liberty but about certainty and control over the future to ensure widespread economic prosperity and, above all, avoidance of war, the essence of which (as de Gaulle was fond of noting) is contingency or chance. ("War is an activity in which the contingent plays an essential part."[42]) Hence, in my view, we might say without distortion that the most fundamental difference between de

Gaulle and Monnet comes down to the importance of preserving the greatest latitude for individual human judgment to deal with "the contingent," a situation best nurtured in de Gaulle's view by states and statesmen and a situation less important in Monnet's eyes than *economic security* over the future. De Gaulle also had more pragmatic differences with those who believed, like Monnet, that they could evolve Europe from low-order "functional integration" (e.g., customs unions) to high order political integration. As de Gaulle said to Malraux of the European Community, "Good luck to this federation without a federator."

De Gaulle's view of the importance of great states also reflects on his view of "history," which for him was not about the progressive elimination of evil on the planet but was made up, rather, in a series of landmark events in the lives and competitions of great civilizations. That is, there is no vestige of millennialism in de Gaulle's statesmanship, even though both his outlook and actions are replete with quasi-religious metaphors concerned with de Gaulle's destiny as the symbolic incarnation of France.[43] Here it is well to let de Gaulle speak for himself on his role in the war:

> When I was an adolescent. . . . I did not doubt that France would have to go through enormous trials, that the whole point of my life consisted of one day rendering her some conspicuous service.[44]

> Among the French . . . the huge convergence of fear, self-interest, and despair brought about a universal abandonment of France. There was not a qualified man in the world who behaved as though he still believed in her independence. . . . When I was faced with the horrifying emptiness of this general desertion, my mission appeared to me in a single flash clear and simple. *At that moment, the worst in her history, it was for me to assume the country's fate, to take France upon myself.*[45]

And, here is de Gaulle writing about himself (like Julius Caesar in the third person but only when the event was of "historic" significance), after the "old regime of parties" reestablished itself in 1946 and he returned to private life:

> Every Frenchman, whatever his tendency, had the troubling suspicion that with the General had vanished *something primordial*, permanent and necessary *which he incarnated in history* and which the regime of parties could not represent.[46]

Whatever this flow called "history" was for de Gaulle[47] is not entirely clear (beyond the interactions of great states and leaders), but it was certainly something he was capable of observing with detachment. As he said of his public *persona:* "De Gaulle interests me only as an historical personality. . ." and "there were many things I would have liked to do but could not for they would not have been fitting for General de Gaulle."[48] History also appears in de Gaulle's eyes to have culminated not in a new Jerusalem but in the end of Western civilization. Here is de Gaulle on this subject near the end of his life to Malraux (sounding very much in tone like Chateaubriand's memoirs, which he mentions he has just been rereading):

> You know as well as I do that Europe will be a compact among States, or nothing. Therefore nothing. We are the last Europeans in Europe, which was Christianity. A tattered Europe, but it did exist. The Europe whose nations hated one another had more reality than the Europe of today.[49]

> I left because of what you were describing a while ago. France was the soul of Christianity—today, let us say, the soul of European civilization. I did all I could to restore her. . . . I tried to prepare France for the end of a certain kind of world. . . . We are certainly witnessing the end of Europe.[50]

> Well, in a few days it will be 1970. . . . Only one generation separates the West from the appearance of the Third World on the stage. In the United States, it is already in position.[51]

DE GAULLE AND THE ART OF STATESMANSHIP IN THE MODERN WORLD

As with Churchill, de Gaulle's achievements reflect unambiguous instances of the arts of statesmanship successfully applied. In both cases we see willful visions, respectively, of a common national good backed by oratorical talent and practical acumen; in both cases we see bearers of these visions performing tasks for their respective countries that, arguably, no other individual could have performed;[52] in both cases we see indifference (even hostility) to partisanship for its own sake. And, in the clashes between these two leaders (and Franklin D. Roosevelt as well), we are reminded that statesmanship involves the rule of *states,* each with its own interests—some of which of necessity will be at odds with those on the "outside," i.e., with other states. We have seen this point especially delineated in the differences between de Gaulle and the European integrationist, Jean Monnet. (To bridge from Plato's *Statesman* to Monnet, we might say in this regard that Monnet's gamble is that the "moderate" in each nation can be made to have more in common with the "moderate" of other nations than with the "spirited" in their own nation. The evolution over three decades of two nuclear super powers certainly encouraged this gamble among certain elites, but has not the dissolution of the Soviet Union now largely removed the "nuclear" constraint upon nationalism?).

Inspection of de Gaulle's public life and career also brings out two aspects of statesmanship that we have not had reason to emphasize heretofore. The first is de Gaulle's emphasis on *governance,* that is, the assertion of legitimate authority to control and regulate a body politic. Coming from a country whose traditions show a long history of political divisiveness (de Gaulle himself characterized the French as capable of lucid thought but unable to act), de Gaulle's authoritative style provided an important element of political stability for his people, a stability codified for future generations in the constitution of the Fifth Republic. From the standpoint of political balance, such an authoritative style would have been misplaced in a more stable political climate such as that of England, as he himself recognized;[53] but for the crises of the third and fourth republics, de Gaulle actually provided what was lacking for political health. As de Gaulle said in defense of his authoritative leadership during the Algerian crisis: "The army only rebels when it is frustrated of its natural instinct to obey."[54]

A second interesting aspect of de Gaulle's statesmanship is the clear understanding it shows of the proper relationship between "theory and practice" or philosophy and political action. (De Gaulle had no use for that monstrous hybrid called "ideology.") By not confusing action and higher thought, de Gaulle always allowed each to be what it was. On this point here is an extremely interesting observation by de Gaulle to Malraux:

> You see, there is something that cannot go on: the irresponsibility of the intellect. Either that will stop or Western civilization will stop. *Intellect* could be concerned with the soul, with the cosmos, as it was for so long. . . . It has concerned itself with temporal life, with politics in the broad sense. *The more it is concerned with politics, the more irresponsible it becomes.*[55]

This sound observation by de Gaulle may be seen as simply a reformulation of Aristotle's insight that if man were the highest being in the cosmos, then politics would be the highest activity.[56] Nor were these simply words on de Gaulle's part. As Lacouture observes, one of de Gaulle's first acts upon entering Paris in 1944 was to renovate and reestablish the Academie Française. As he confided to a poet in this period, "I believe that France is regaining her power. But what she needs now is serenity."[57] And, of course, unlike Woodrow Wilson and other millennialists, de Gaulle never attempted the misguided project of marshalling partial insights of reason behind political action to redeem the world. Rather de Gaulle always attempted to hold up to his countrymen and women their neoclassical heritage to move them in the direction of balance and moderation (mesure).[58]

7

Richard Nixon and Henry Kissinger

I TAKE THE CASES OF RICHARD NIXON AND HIS NATIONAL SECURITY adviser (later secretary of state) Henry Kissinger as a team,[1] because while neither may have achieved greatness, together they present interesting subject matter for our analysis of statesmanship, providing examples in the age of nuclear weapons and television. In addition both have written a great deal (by comparison with other contemporaries) about statesmen and statesmanship.[2] As with our previous subjects, my primary aim will not be to provide a comprehensive judgment on their title to "statesmanship" but to use their words and deeds to illustrate aspects of the art of statesmanship. (Even Nixon's most perceptive and articulate defender to date, English historian Paul Johnson, is explicit on the impossibility of indicating what the historical judgment on the Nixon presidency will be.[3])

Important issues to be analyzed here still appear very varied because of their proximity to us after only two decades, but, *for our purposes,* I have compacted them into two major ones. The first issue has to do with understanding the nature of power (and its various mutations) in the international arena during the decades of "nuclear terror" between the United States and the (former) Soviet Union. The second has to do with the power of the television (and other) press (and more generally, public opinion) in advanced democracy and how it should be handled from the standpoint of statesmanship. In my view, and as I shall try to show, the Nixon-Kissinger legacy shows insightfulness (with exceptions) on the first question, and Nixon's misfortunes can largely be explained in terms of the second. The Vietnam War may be seen as an instance of the convergence of the two influences, as I shall illustrate.

One of the themes of this book has been about the dangers for the art of statesmanship in millennialist attempts to alter the fundamental structure of political relations involving, as one of its components, the use (or at least threat) of coercion and/or armed force. Although Kissinger's fascination with Kant[4] (in combination with his ties to the North-eastern intellectual establishment) may have made him more susceptible to this fallacy than Nixon, still he never fully succumbed to it.[5] (Even when offering the Soviets huge concessions to keep alive at least the appearance of *detente* in the early 1970s, it is difficult to believe Kissinger really expected to be successful—this was simply the program of the Republican eastern wing whose support he did not wish to lose, above all.[6])

The form that this millennialist project appeared in during the forty-five years from the Soviet development of nuclear weapons to the dissolution of the Soviet Union was called "arms control." Understood comprehensively to include its esoteric meanings, the phrase came to denote not merely efforts to restrain the development and production of nuclear weapons but something akin to an ideology or theology to replace traditional conceptions of international relations since Thucydides. Conceived initially as a way of stably asserting national interests in a bipolar nuclear world by configuring nuclear arms in certain patterns,[7] it came over time to imply (in its broadest connotations[8]) a model for an ongoing process of negotiation between the super powers under a nuclear balance of terror, which permitted the limited use of force in "local wars" while guaranteeing hypothetical mutual destruction in the event of escalation into nuclear war. Its implications for the arts of statesmanship and politics involved its effects on national sovereignty and on the role of even one's own military forces, which were seen as potential disrupters of peace (the model's overriding goal) between the super powers. Although the model's policy influence was not substantially curtailed until the Reagan administration,[9] Nixon, and to some extent Kissinger, did attempt to resist it while in office, and in subsequent writings both are critical of its assumptions. Kissinger is interesting here, especially, because he flirted with the model and its assumptions during his years at Harvard. Here is a "retraction" he made in Brussels in 1979 (at the end of the Carter presidency, when the U.S. strategic position was considered vulnerable to a Soviet counterforce strike by SS-18 missiles):

> Since the middle 1960s the growth of the Soviet strategic force has been massive. . . . And the amazing phenomenon about which histori-

ans will ponder is that all of this happened without the United States attempting to rectify that state of affairs. *One . . . reason was the growth of a school of thought to which I, myself, contributed . . .* in which the amazing theory developed, i.e., historically amazing, that vulnerability contributed to peace and invulnerability contributed to the risks of war.

Such a theory could develop and be widely accepted only in a country that had never addressed the problem of the balance of power as a historical phenomenon. . . . It was a general theory that suffered two drawbacks.

One was that the Soviets did not believe it.[10]

An interesting question for our analysis is how the Nixon-Kissinger administration dealt with aspects of this comprehensive ideology,[11] which, as I have noted, included prescriptions for the (non)use of force down to "limited wars" such as what occurred in Vietnam.[12] In the interest of a manageable analysis, let us look at the issues of nuclear arms levels, the anti-ballistic missile program (an attempt at limiting vulnerability), and the handling of the Vietnam war.

In the second volume of his memoirs, Kissinger lists the difficulties facing the Nixon administration (conservative hostility to arms control, eroding presidential authority following the Watergate revelations,[13] liberal opposition to Nixon himself—whatever the issue, a relentless Soviet arms build up, liberal support for arms control as an end in itself, congressional resistance to any increase in the defense budget) and then makes the following claim:

> The Nixon Administration deserves great credit for having preserved the sinews of our defense in the face of a relentless Congressional and media assault. Every new strategic program in existence a decade later . . . had its origin under the stewardship of Nixon and Ford.[14]

The burden of Kissinger's argument is that the "strategic balance" vis-à-vis the Soviets under Breshnev would have been worse—given the political climate in the United States—if the Nixon administration had not engaged in arms control agreements and efforts at detente. Furthermore, he argues that the liberal view of arms control as an end in itself, and of the necessity of ensuring our own vulnerability (M.A.D.) as a basis for stability in the nuclear age, would have been even more entrenched if the Nixon administration had not attempted (a largely unsuccessful) detente with the Soviet Union. Let us leave comment on this latter issue for a moment and focus on the claim that, given the Soviet concentration on a massive counterforce capability (through use of multiple warheads on new generations of increasingly accurate, large missiles), the "strategic imbalance" would have been worse without the administration's efforts to preserve the "sinews of our defense." Overall this seems to me a defensible assertion—given the unfavorable U.S. domestic political climate—with one important exception. This was the congressional decision to scrap the one antiballistic missile system we actually had in place in North Dakota. If the Nixon administration was really so opposed (as Kissinger implies) to the idea of stability through increased vulnerability, then this was a decision that should have been more strenuously resisted. Let us recall the facts.

The Nixon administration inherited from the Johnson administration an ongoing project for population defense, which it restructured for purposes of missile defense instead. The new project came to be known as the "Safeguard" system and originally was to include twelve sites. In arms control agreements with the Soviets, the administration came to the stipulation that each country would have only two sites; then in 1974, only one site was stipulated. In 1975, with no strenuous opposition from President Ford, Kissinger, or the Pentagon,[15] an amendment passed both the Senate and House to dismantle the one Safeguard site (less its radar) in operation at Grand Forks, North Dakota. Thus the only operational ballistic missile defense system that the United States has ever had (to this day), and which was permitted under our own agreements with the Soviet Union, came to an end, for "budgetary reasons" according to Kissinger in his memoirs.[16]

The reasons for this decision were complex[17] and included its symbolic value as an index of increased vulnerability, public hostility following the Vietnam War to the very idea of defense, decreased defense appropriations, and the fact that new generations of multiple warheaded Soviet missiles (MIRVs) were held to have rendered the Safeguard system's effectiveness highly problematic. However arms control opponents have always criticized the decision,[18] which symbolized the triumph of the assured destruction school of deterrence until President Reagan's speech on strategic defense during his first term in office. More concretely the decision resulted in the dismantling of the only operational system the United States has ever had that might be used to stop an incoming intercontinental ballistic missile, even one launched by accident or by a "renegade" nuclear power.

Because the aim here is to evaluate the Nixon-Kissinger administration's handling of the "arms control-mutual assured destruction ideology," let us look at their reasoning on the Safeguard missile defense decision. Although, as we have seen, Kissinger later expressed his doubts about the idea of stability through mutual vulnerability[19] (especially since the Soviets never accepted it), at the time he did not. Nixon and Kissinger both viewed the Safeguard system as a "bargaining chip" with the Soviet Union in arms control talks, and Nixon cites the agreement (without protest) on the ABM system as acceptance of the system of "mutual terror."[20]

Their approach suggests that for both Nixon and Kissinger the issue was always seen through the prism of *political* power,[21] domestically and vis-à-vis negotiations with the Soviet Union. Thus, had he been in office in 1975, it is conceivable Nixon might have chosen to oppose the decision to dismantle Safeguard (especially because the amendment came from Senator Edward Kennedy), but he would have done so out of considerations of his own power and authority as president not from an attempt to ascertain the implications for national sovereignty, or war-fighting, or out of any consideration that had not entered the terms of political debate in the relevant forum, domestic or international. Thus, to take our bearings from this telling incident, it does not appear that Nixon (unlike his heroes Churchill and de Gaulle) could have provided the kind of statesmanship that looks deeper into national problems than their likely effects on conventionally construed (however imaginatively so) power relations and hence could probably not have led his country out of a *great* crisis or forestalled one. And, on the same point and incident, if Kissinger is capable of analysis that penetrates more deeply into problems than their conventionally construed political formulations, it is not clear from his record that he is prepared to *act* on his analyses when they take him very far outside the views of his political and social supporters of the moment.[22]

Another perspective on how the Nixon-Kissinger administration dealt with the "ideology of arms control-coercive diplomacy" can be had from inspection of their handling of the war in South Vietnam. As I have tried to show elsewhere,[23] the strategy of nuclear deterrence through magnified vulnerability had given birth to a view of the use of all armed force (in the nuclear age) as a matter of bargaining over increments of pain inflicted or with-held.[24] This outlook provided a basis for the "internal mutation" of military tactics (at the most basic levels) *away from* the logic of war winning based on traditional capabilities to ward-off, close with and defeat and *toward* the limitation of even conventional military force from within its own logic. (This approach is to be distinguished from the limitation of the Korean conflict by direct imposition of presidential authority in discrete instances.) The issue here from the standpoint of statesmanship, in my view, has to do with the likely and actual effects of this outlook on the American military profession and, in turn, on the American liberal democracy.

One of Kissinger's Harvard colleagues, Samuel Huntington, had written a book on the American civil-military relations (in 1957, the same year that Kissinger's *Nuclear Weapons and Foreign Policy* appeared), which asserted that, given the selfishness and self-interest of this commercial democracy, the antidote or hope for civic balance lay in what American society had to learn from duty-oriented West Point (not vice versa) and that, if the American officer corps ever "abjured the military spirit," it would destroy itself and, in time, the nation.[25] This is the general issue I wish to take up here, though I find Huntington vague on one major point. As I see it the issue involves not the "destruction" of the nation but a regime change (to speak the language of political theory) from a republic to an imperial democracy or simple empire.[26] That is, the economic view of warfare articulated at the Harvard Center for International Affairs in the late 1950s and early 1960s (as a matter of trading increments of pain for marginal political gains) took its bearings from eighteenth-century limited war between depostically led mercenary forces and tended, in turn, to create the same kind of relationship (albeit in diluted form) between American political leadership and American military leadership, many of whom felt that their profession had been betrayed in the Vietnam War.[27] (Today, certainly, a very plausible case can be made that owing to the effects of the McNamara era and the now authoritative view that deterrence is a component of defense, rather than vice versa,[28] Huntington's 1957 characterization of the American military *ethos* is simply no longer relevant to an officer corps of predominantly corporate military managers.[29])

Now the question for our analysis is whether Nixon and Kissinger saw this issue in their handling of the Vietnam War or, even if they did, gave it much weight in their mutual view of the imperatives and opportunities for "creative statesmanship" that the various world crises of the 1970s provided.[30] The answer in Kissinger's case is more complex than for Nixon, because Kissinger admittedly contributed to the influential "ideology" I am describing. In fact Kissinger has a paragraph in *Nuclear Weapons and Foreign Policy* (1957) implying a conception of limited war based on what I have called the "internal mutation" of the military profession and its skills:

> The more the military plan on the basis of crushing the enemy even in a limited area, the more the political leadership will recoil before the risk of taking *any* military action. The more limited war is conceived of as a "small" all-out war, the more it will produce inhibitions similar to those generated by the concept of massive retaliation.[31]

Kissinger's implication is clearly that the traditional military aims of warding off and defeating enemy forces is too risky (at any level) in the nuclear age to be politically viable and that some alternative (e.g., war as bargaining over punitive increments) susceptible to direct manipulation by political leadership is called for. But even if Kissinger's writings had an important influence (along with other intellectuals at Harvard and Princeton) on the Kennedy (and Johnson) administration's policies in Vietnam, how are we to judge him, and Nixon, on the actual conduct of the war, once they had inherited it and the responsibilities of office?

It has been asserted that Kissinger engineered a defeat in Vietnam (which has left a scar on the American national psyche) as part of his plan for a new global order to replace the old containment system.[32] But this is surely unfair. Although Kissinger may have contributed to the formation of intellectual models that influenced the Kennedy administration's "defense" policies, it is the Kennedy and Johnson administrations that bear the responsibility for the judgment to enter and fight a war (with American troops and financial deficits) that had no clear and decisive connection between military means and political ends. In the context of an American nation with neither the will nor the economic surplus to continue the struggle, the Nixon-Kissinger administration was simply trying to withdraw without endangering what had been achieved in a decade's efforts and sacrifices. The final collapse of South Vietnam before a massed North Vietnamese armored invasion was an immediate consequence of a huge Soviet increase in the quantity and quality of aid to North Vietnam, coupled with a huge American decrease in aid to South Vietnam.[33] Nor, in my view, can the disintegration of American will to continue be attributed primarily to the Nixon administration's temporary widening of maneuvers into Cambodia and Laos to secure conditions for the safe withdrawal of American troops. The Nixon administration was simply acting out a script written by the Kennedy administration and its academic advisers, which, in the overriding interest of deterring the mobilization of national will in the nuclear age, was prepared to employ American troops (and conscripts) in a fashion intended (as one of its goals[34]) to divide the nation between the "spirited" and the "moderate." And the issue for statesmanship is whether the choice of a few Americans to use many other Americans in this manner did not nurture—to speak again the language of political theory—imperial over republican regime principles. In my view, on the Vietnam question, the Nixon-Kissinger administration did about the best that could have been done in the very bad situation they inherited.

One of the contributing factors in the disintegration of American domestic support for the war was the role played by television in reporting the war and characterizing the administration's aims.[35] Inspection of this problem serves as a bridge to another general issue for statesmanship in advanced, modern democracy—how to deal with the power of public opinion multiplied (and to some extent generated) by television technology. To what extent did the Nixon-Kissinger administration recognize and manage this phenomenon?

As I see it there are three analytically separable issues here. One is the power of public opinion in democracy; another is the role of newspapers and "the print media" in the formation of public opinion; and the last is the power of television in the formation and reflection of public opinion in a democracy. Clearly, given the power of public opinion in the openness of democracy, a requirement of statesmanship is to listen to it, to learn from it when it has something to teach, and to educate and constrain its less constructive impulses when possible. Above all else the task of statesmanship in this context is not to allow widely held mistaken judgments (owing to lack of timely information, lack of perspective, selfishness, loss of nerve) to diminish the prestige, authority, and skill necessary for governmental leadership to do what is best for the long-range interests of the country as a whole.

Yet this is exactly a danger that afflicts advanced democracy, so much so that one book on statesmanship explicitly suggests that (owing to its love of equality and openness) democracy is in tension with the very idea of statesmanship.[36] As has often been observed, television magnifies and intensifies the phenomenon of public opinion in democratic governance (and foreign policy!) through timely and largely unmediated transmission of near and distant images to huge numbers of people simultaneously, some of whom have never thought or reflected about the events whose electronic images are suddenly before their eyes. Perhaps more than any other medium of communication, televised images are susceptible to being taken "out of context" while simultaneously generating widespread and firm convictions of having grasped "the real reality" of a situation ("seeing is believing!"). This is especially so in inherently dramatic instances, such as the use of force and violence or the depiction of extreme physical deprivation.

The case we have just considered in another context—the circumstances of American withdrawal from the Vietnam war—is illustrative of this general phenomenon. Nixon himself has written on this score that "the one-sided coverage television gave the war in Vietnam was probably the single most significant factor in so limiting our options that the war was lengthened and ultimately lost."[37]

The most dramatic and decisive instance that comes to mind in this context is the newspaper and television coverage of the 1968 "Tet Offensive." This event, treated as a Viet Cong victory by the American press,[38] is often taken as a "watershed" event in the disintegration of public support for the war, yet as is now well documented, the outcome of the offensive was a massive diminution of Viet Cong numbers necessitating take over of the war effort by North Vietnamese regulars for the duration.[39] More generally it is clear that nightly depiction of scenes of suffering and death year upon year had complicated effects upon American viewers, one of which was arguably to instill a *sense of guilt* in those at home in the "Great Society" who were making no sacrifices (not even economic ones) *toward* combatants on both sides. (The effects of such coverage are now fairly well known, so much so that the Bush administration took careful steps vis-à-vis the press to prevent their likely reoccurrence during the 1990 Gulf war with Iraq.) But what was the Nixon-Kissinger approach to the press and television press coverage, that arguably brought down the Nixon White House by generating and sustaining the Watergate scandal?[40]

The Nixon administration is especially interesting in this regard, given Nixon's long history of contention with, and open contempt for, the American press. Additionally both Nixon and Kissinger were averse to making policy (not to mention "creative" foreign policy designed to alter the world order) by majoritarian consensus, open to all eyes.[41] Nixon also was clearly aware of the general effects of television on uncritical viewers. Here is his own characterization:

> Television . . . changes the way people see things and events. Like a mind-altering drug, which in a very real sense it is, it distorts their perception of reality. The neat little capsule dramas that we see on the screen . . . are not mirrors of life. They are distorting mirrors. . . . The line between fact and fantasy is blurred into invisibility, and increasingly the public accepts this blurring.[42]

Yet, in spite of his appreciation of its power to influence public perceptions, Nixon and his White House staff operated in open defiance of the television (and other) press, making foreign policy primarily based on substantive considerations about long-range, U.S. interests; in the end that press brought Nixon down. What is the lesson to be learned here from the standpoint of statesmanship in democracy? One putative lesson (learned especially well by Ronald Reagan) is to try to beat television at its own game, by assimilating its techniques for mass, symbolic communication and preempting their use. (But there are another set of dangers in this approach, as we know.) Another lesson might be that American democracy occasionally requires leaders willing to oppose its predominant opinions and subsequently be sacrificed to its wrath. (But this is not a solution that can be planned beforehand, if it not to bring into high office unstable, Romantic influences.) In my view the general lesson here for the future practice of statesmanship has to do with discerning a real, practical danger facing the American democracy in the television age. This danger involves a dubious division of labor between leaders and the majority of citizens and can be glimpsed in dramatic form in the propaganda methods employed in the 1930s on the German people. It involves the use of mass communication techniques and devices to convey simple, vague, symbolic images (designed to produce uniform emotional states in audiences) that are addressed to no particular objects or policies. Leaders can then use these simultaneously induced emotional states to manipulate largely transparent populations in the direction of outcomes that they intend to achieve. Such a situation, as its grows, produces not only an unhealthy division of labor between managers of desired outcomes and the population that places them in office to achieve these specific outcomes, but leads as well to a form of public debate that is largely meaningless (on its intellectual merits) except as an indicator of what specific outcomes a potential officeholder favors or opposes. Said differently television's capacity to reduce complex realities to a few, simple images and disseminate them rapidly, repeatedly, and ubiquitously strengthens a tendency currently afoot to sever the link *between* widespread informed and reasoned judgment *and* support for particular programs and policies—a link that distinguishes a balanced and healthy democratic republic from a benignly despotic one.[43]

Hence the lesson for future statesmanship in this context—whether the choice is to defy the television press as did Nixon or beat it at its own game as did Reagan (and as Clinton is attempting to do)—involves above all else recognition of the long-range dangers to civic balance inherent in the widespread use of television and a willingness to take these into account in choosing any particular approach to dealing with it. In fact the ability of high officeholders to stay on top of media events, while retaining the intent to do what is best for civic balance of the body politic in the long run, provides a major test of statesmanship in the context of the television dilemma.

NIXON, KISSINGER, AND STATESMANSHIP

I have tried to show that the Nixon-Kissinger administration displayed statesmanlike qualities in resisting two unhealthy and divisive tendencies afoot in American democracy. One was the tendency to move toward an imperial-like treatment and use of our armed forces, made intellectually legitimate for many through an economic approach to warfare (which Kissinger contributed to in his writings while at Harvard in the 1950s and

1960s). The other was (and is) the tendency of the television media to divide public policy debate in the United States into a realm of simple, vague images and symbols for public consumption on the one hand and a discrete realm of technical detail for leaders and policy makers on the other, with little intellectual (versus emotional) link between the two. In connection with resistance to this latter tendency, there is another statesmanlike quality in the Nixon-Kissinger legacy that has been present throughout our analysis, but which I have not yet made explicit, that is, its emphasis on the written word and on reflection about the requirements of statesmanship itself.

If the highest task of statesmanship is to govern the relationship of political life to thought and reflection[44] and if the American polity assigns this task to the people themselves, then in our system more than any other a major task of statesmanship is to enlighten and instruct. On this score Nixon and Kissinger receive high marks, both for their recognition of this duty and (in most cases) for the content of their writings, both in and out of office. Here is what one author has to say about the quality and depth of policy explanation during the Nixon-Kissinger years:

> Although policy was made less openly during the Nixon-Kissinger year than before, the rationales for policies received greater articulation than in any other presidency. The "State of the World" messages that Nixon sent to Congress . . . and Kissinger's briefings as NSC adviser . . . and congressional testimony as secretary of state, cannot be viewed as mere political justifications for policies. Kissinger attempted to explain the underlying philosophy that had led to a particular policy choice.[45]

In my view this judgment is correct in its essentials and lends support to the claim that the best gift to the art of statesmanship of the Nixon-Kissinger legacy is its dramatic recognition (in a highly unreflective age) of the intimacy of reflection and action connoted by the very idea of this art. That is, if one unhealthy tendency of democracy is to move toward a public realm of mere "sight" and "appearance," for that is what *all* can grasp as meaningful, and if widespread use of television exacerbates this tendency, then a function of statesmanship in the service of civic balance is to resist it by nurturing a fuller and deeper grasp of political and other reality within the civic body. To this end Nixon and Kissinger contributed, both in and out of office.

8

The Modern Challenges to Statesmanship

THIS BOOK BEGAN WITH A STATEMENT OF THE SALIENT MODERN challenges to the Aristotelian and Ciceronian ideas of statesmanship and oratory and followed with an exploration of the public careers of several modern leaders, beginning with George Washington. The aim was to see what light inspection of the words and deeds of practicing statesmen might shed on resolution of the tensions between an ancient pagan ideal and the challenges posed to it by Christianity in its various evolving forms, by the modern state, by modern liberalism, and by modern science and technology, to name the major ones. My aim now is *not* a prosaic rehearsal of those features of our individual case studies which qualify as statesmanlike but rather a general statement of those aspects of statesmanship that must endure if the term is any longer to describe a meaningful practical activity or art.

In my view the essence of statesmanship, in any age, is the concrete, practical activity of creating and/or nurturing the general conditions for politics to occur as the *primary* basis for human life together. The meaning of politics is central here, for that is what statesmanship works to achieve, and it is the medium through which it leads, influences, and reconciles differences. Implicit in Aristotle's designation of the "middle-class" regime (of citizens capable of the common defense) as *the political polity*[1] is the idea that politics is the moderate solution to living together[2] and that it evolved in its purest form among "middling" persons dependent on one another to get on but not so dependent as to wish to be managed by a permanent clique of rulers.[3] (This does not mean that there was not great statesmanship in aristocratic societies but that it was not as political a form as can occur under republics and democratic republics—the Platonic view to the contrary notwithstanding.)

For politics to occur, the conditions for moderation must be

118

present and must endure against immoderation and extremism. (Obviously, then, one of the greatest tasks of statesmanship is to create such conditions out of adverse circumstances, whether utopian or barbaric.) A necessity for the achievement of sustained moderation—as I have tried to show in our various case studies—is the capacity of rulers and ruled to recognize the "structure of political reality," in particular two of its abiding features. These features are abiding not because human nature is unmalleable, but because if they are denied, the outcomes will not be, carefully speaking, political. These features are reliance on artful, persuasive utterance and reliance on the threat (and sometimes use) of coercion and armed force.

By themselves these features of politics cannot generate statesmanship, an art that requires more positive capacities to lead and inspire unity for objects of general good. But their absence, or the willful intent to use traditional political means to eliminate them, will, over time, eliminate possibilities for the practice of statesmanship by diminishing the possibilities for politics, understood as a web of institutions and practices for the moderate reconciliation of differences and the achievement of objects of public good. On this view, then, the greatest threats to the art of statesmanship in the modern world have come not from liberalism's reduction of the scope of the political realm, or its compartmentalization of various spheres of activity, but from millennialist and quasi-millennialist attempts to eliminate or radically minimize the influence of the of the two aforementioned structural features of political reality, often in the name of liberating greater numbers of people from conditions of oppression and poverty. (The problem is, to borrow a phrase from Michael Oakeshott, that the poor may have far more to lose than their poverty.)

Our various case studies, in different ways, shed light on this problem. From the standpoint of the balanced integration of the ideals of western liberalism (as well as the good possibilities of modern technology) and the abiding political requirements for continued moderation, Washington and Churchill must be considered our best instances. Washington, even when convinced of the historical destiny of this nation, never showed confusion about the differences between the realms of the immanent and the transcendent (not even in the "Farewell Address" drafted by Hamilton, laying a basis for American "exceptionalism"). In my view this was not simply because of Washington's proximity to the "Enlightenment"—which has been quite influential in millennialist schemes—but, if anything, because of his proximity to European aristocracy, whose errors have rarely been in the democratic directions of pantheism and immanentism.[4] And Churchill achieved, as we have seen, many progressive and liberal aims pragmatically, with a deep and sound understanding of the differences between political reality and millennialist hopes.

The cases of Lincoln and de Gaulle strike me as more ambiguous vis-à-vis the standards of our analysis. Lincoln's leadership eliminated a great evil in the American system—chattel slavery— but at the expense of a sound understanding of constitutionalism in the electorate at large[5] and by nurturing American millennialist impulses, which Woodrow Wilson, in turn, exacerbated. General de Gaulle, in my view, showed his limits in holding too rigidly to pagan (Roman) standards of authority, which, while not a millennialist error to be sure, did not make him a great leader (unlike Churchill) except when his country was in need of spirited defense whether against external aggression or domestic factiousness. (However, in one such moment de Gaulle bequeathed France a stable, constitutional mixture of order and stability that still supports it.)

The case of Woodrow Wilson I have cited as our purest instance of millennialism, a direct attack upon what I have called "the structure of political reality," through the use of traditional political means. If Wilson was able to mobilize the American people against an overbearing corporate oligarchy, which arguably threatened their civic balance, a long-range effect of his infusion of religious and eschatalogical motifs directly into American political life has arguably been to generate a pervasive and imbalanced atheistic reaction against religion anywhere in its public life. And if the corporate oligarchy he felt called to combat ensconced itself as a consequence of Lincoln's millennialist war (as Lincoln himself predicted it would[6]), then the political stability of the American people appears precarious in the long run, absent a better explicit understanding[7] of the arts of statesmanship and politics to rescue them from such pendulum swings.

Finally the case of Nixon and Kissinger, while not an instance of greatness, was analyzed as illustrative of resistance to the potentially millennialist tendencies of an influential paradigm for national security in the nuclear age (which it is true Kissinger had helped to formulate in his academic days). And, as I tried to show

on another score, the emphasis of both men on the written word
and on reflection about statesmanship itself is important in a re-
ductivist television age in resisting a new set of dangers for the
art of statesmanship.

Because I have suggested that one of the features of statesmanship is recognition of the "intimacy of reflection and action" inherent in the very idea of this art,[8] perhaps a fitting way of
concluding this exploration is to reflect more deeply on the abiding features of political reality already mentioned. First take the
relationship of politics to armed force. My point is not that of von
Clausewitz (and Carl Schmitt[9]) that war is a continuation of politics
and policy by other means. In fact this formulation seems to me
inaccurate in its blurring of the differences between the political
threat or anticipation of force and its (extrapolitical) actual application. Nor is my point the Weberian one that because politics is
(putatively) merely the striving to share power, the state is simply
the institution that successfully claims a monopoly of the legitimate means of violence. As a matter of logic, Weber's definition
cannot distinguish the state from an army, nor politics from force.
My commonsense point is that the capability to use force skillfully
in a military fashion externally, and in a police fashion internally,
constitutes a precondition for the meaningful use of persuasive
means in reconciling and achieving consensus on policy. The difference between the use of force in a politically related fashion
from mere violence or sporadic use of force is its relationship or
link to the authority of a body politic and its state. The conduct
of politics and the use of political means presupposes an authoritative context that distinguishes between those on the outside and
those on the inside[10] as the very basis for the moderation of means
available to insiders (i.e., citizens). And even on the "inside," police
force and its threat are used to constrain and contain civil distur-
bances and criminal acts against life and property. If there were
ever the realistic possibility of sustained reliance on moderate
means of persuasion without the credible threat of armed force
to carve out a realm for it, then, as utopians such as the young
Marx foresaw, politics and the state might indeed "wither away"
without the passing of freedom and moderation as well.

Yet it is not merely (as Marx thought) the intensity of competition for resources and reputation that leads to the need for armed
force in creating "spaces" for moderation. (Nor is it merely the

misperceptions and actual dangers arising from our mutual inse-
curities, as Hobbes chose to emphasize.) It is rather that political
authority, shored up by the capability for skillful use of armed
force, provides a kind of "short-hand" to create the "slack" for
reasoned judgment and deliberation over courses of action, which
technology and mere economic surpluses are incapable of generating by themselves. (For these latter threaten *to transform citizens,*
possessing the latitude, leisure, and detachment to deliberate, *into*
industrious role-performers in a never-ending, collective enterprise of great magnitude. This is to say that the threat and occasional use of force is a way of keeping both one's own citizen body,
as well as its potential enemies, "honest," without taking away the
freedom and distance for them to reflect about general political
and social courses of action. This is perhaps the element of truth
in the old adage that "an armed society is a polite society.")

The corollary of such misguided expectations about the super-
fluity of armed force in the creation of regional "spaces" for the
practice of moderation is a blindness about another form of
"short-hand" in the human psychic economy—the use of rhetoric
and artfully persuasive utterance in generating cooperation and
even occasional consensus. The utopian expectation here is that
the realm of political discourse may be displaced by a realm of
"discursive ethics" or "ideal speech situations,"[11] in which the rational pursuit of truth[12] displaces the old politics of compromise
and accommodation. However, even if a sufficient number of persons could be found willing to undertake such a utopian experiment, they would encounter the same general problem as those
hoping to dispense with the threat and use of force—loss of the
distance, perspective, and leisure finally to act. This "truth experiment" would become an endless and laborious process that at
some point would either psychologically coerce a consensus or
simply proclaim *ex cathedra* some particular interest as the general
interest. This project resembles the Wilsonian attempt to eliminate the gap between individual and political ethics, except that
it would displace individual with collective decision making, and
it is, thus, more realistic (and more open) about the need for
some coercion.

Another danger for the continued practice of deliberation and
artful persuasion over general courses of action was discussed in
the Nixon-Kissinger chapter. It involves the use of television to
simplify and repeat and to transmit electronically vague images

and symbols to huge audiences simultaneously. The dangers it poses for the arts of statesmanship and politics are not utopian but rather benignly despotic. Rather than nurturing habits of political judgment (bridging from general principles to particular policies), its general effect is to engender vague emotional states—directed to no particular objects—in its audiences. The persuasive links are blurred *between* the reasons for policies *and* the choice of policies or even grand courses of action. Instead public discourse becomes more a matter of transmitting symbolic images which convey to audiences the specific policy outcomes a potential (or actual) policy-maker favor. Strategies for dealing with the television phenomenon were discussed in the previous chapter, but I mention the general problem again to illustrate the point that threats to conditions for the practice of statesmanship and politics come from antirationalist as well as ultra-rationalist tendencies and forces.

Summary

At the risk of prosaic repetition, let us briefly rehearse this book's central argument. Statesmanship in the modern world of the past four centuries was seen to have important affinities with the ancient ideals that animated its modern practitioners like Washington, Churchill, and de Gaulle. Although they lived and acted in a public world that defines itself in terms of *relationships* rather than abiding *essences,* their careers illustrate the point that parts of especially the Aristotelian account of statesmanship or political rule can be meaningfully restated for practice in modern language. In my own attempt at this restatement, statesmanship has been seen as an activity directed toward securing the conditions for politics to occur, as the basis for agreement about general courses of action, and for moderate reconciliation of differences among fellow citizens. This art requires, in addition to the capability to inspire convictions of unity in a body politic, the quality of prudence, understood as intelligence about the abiding features of political action in whatever novel circumstances. Finally this book has implied throughout that this art, insofar as it involves governing and nurturing the conditions for politics to occur, will remain important for as long as politics[13] is recognized to be the most choice-worthy of alternatives upon which to base human life in common—a most problematic prospect in an age beguiled by various forms of tender-mindedness united in their hostility to greatness and to the political and moral ideals and abstractions[14] necessary for it to arise and be sought after.

Notes

INTRODUCTION

1. For an "infamous" instance of contemporary academic debate over the irrelevance/relevance of ancient political theory for modern political practice, see Stephen Taylor Holmes, "Aristippus in and out of Athens" and the reply to it by James H. Nichols, Jr. in the *American Political Science Review* 73 no. 1 (March 1979), 113–33. Neither writer explicitly addresses the contention of this book that at the highest levels of leadership during intense crises, the ancient viewpoint is demonstrably more applicable than in normal times for average citizens of pluralist democracies. See also on this general subject Appendix A ("Two Views of Aristotle's *Politics*") of Wendell J. Coats, Jr., *A Theory of Republican Character and Related Essays* (London and Toronto: Associated University Presses, 1994), 147–57.

2. This issue is discussed in the chapter on Washington, but for a quick summary of the contending viewpoints, see Richard Loss, "The Political Thought of George Washington," *Presidential Studies Quarterly* 19, no. 3 (Summer 1989), 482–83. See also, Cicero, *De Officiis*, 2, 21–22, trans. Walter Miller (Cambridge, Mass.: Harvard University Press/Loeb Classical Library), 249–55.

3. See, on the issue of "intensity," n. 9 to chap. 8.

4. To extend the thought by stating the obvious, such decisions influence in turn, more and less strongly, the shape of the historical inheritance with which future leaders must contend and work. Hence it is as misleading to assert that the lives of complex, pluralist societies are largely impervious to the directing influence of the long-range decisions of high political leadership as it is to assert that modern statesmanship is analogous to a *techne* molding otherwise inert "citizen-matter."

CHAPTER 1. FROM ANCIENT WRITERS TOWARD A THEORY OF MODERN STATESMANSHIP

1. Edith Hamilton and Huntington Cairns, eds., *The Collected Dialogues of Plato* (Princeton: Princeton University Press, 1963), 1062–63, 2936–3.

2. Ibid., 1075, 304a.

3. Ibid., 1077, 305d–e.

4. Ibid., 1080, 307e–308a.

5. Ibid., 1082, 309d.

6. Ernest Baker, ed., *The Politics of Aristotle* (London: Oxford University Press, 1958), Book 1, 1–38, 1252a–1259b.

7. Ibid., 105, 1277b16.

8. Ibid., 104–5, 1277b13–14. On some implications of political rule for con-

temporary political practice, see Mary P. Nichols, *Citizens and Statesmen: A Study of Aristotle's Politics* (Savage, Md.: Rowman & Littlefield Publishers, Inc., 1992), especially 5: "Aristotle does justice to both . . . democratic and aristocratic aspirations through his concept of political rule or statesmanship. Political rule or statesmanship for Aristotle is rule by virtuous individuals that nevertheless requires for its success the participation of the people. Statesmanship is impossible without citizenship."

9. Michael Grant, ed., *Cicero on the Good Life* (London: Penguin Books, 1971), 289.

10. Cicero, *De Officiis*, The Loeb Classical Library (Cambridge: Harvard University Press, 1913), 241, para. 66.

11. Matt., 22:21; Mark, 12:17.

12. St. Augustine, *The City of God Against the Pagans*, The Loeb Classical Library, vol. 6 (Cambridge: Harvard University Press, 1960), 195.

13. Ibid., 197–98.

14. For development of this theme, see Herbert A. Deane, *The Political and Social Ideas of St. Augustine* (New York: Columbia University Press, 1963), 221–243.

15. The full phrase to describe this Thomist view is "gratia non tollit naturam, sed perficit."

16. For development of the theme that modern liberalism develops out of Protestant Christianity, one could see (besides Hegel), G. de Ruggiero, *The History of European Liberalism*, trans. R. G. Collingwood (Oxford: Oxford University Press, 1927).

17. Niccolo Machiavelli, *The Prince*, trans. George Bull (New York: Penguin Books 1961), 91.

18. Ibid., 94–95.

19. Ibid., 96.

20. Ibid., 101.

21. Cicero, *De Officiis*, 287.

22. Ibid., 299.

23. Ibid., 297.

24. Ibid., 369.

25. Winston Churchill, *The Gathering Storm*, vol. 1 of *The Second World War* (Boston: Houghton Mifflin Company, 1948), 287–88.

26. Ibid., 288.

27. H. H. Gerth and C. Wright Mills, eds., *From Max Weber* (New York: Oxford University Press, 1958), 126.

28. Ibid., 126.

29. Michael B. Foster, *The Political Philosophies of Plato and Hegel* (Oxford: Clarendon Press, 1935), 187.

30. Ibid., 187–88.

31. C. Rubin and L. Rubin, eds., *The Quest for Justice* (Lexington, Mass.: Ginn Publishing, 1984), 166.

32. For a discriminating treatment of this problem, see P. T. Bauer, *Dissent on Development*, rev. ed. (Cambridge: Harvard University Press, 1976).

33. On this point Machiavelli says that we may fall from power through lack of skill, but we may not extend our time in power past what is ordained by fortune through possession of skill; however, because we can never know in advance when our time has passed, we should always employ our skills as though

it were not yet. Niccolo Machiavelli, *Discourses on the First Ten Books of Livy*, Book 2, chapter 29, any edition.

34. These are maxims from a recent "manual" by Christopher Matthews, entitled *Hardball: How Politics Is Played Told by One Who Knows the Game* (New York: Harper and Row, 1988).

35. T. Harry Williams, *Huey Long* (New York: Vintage Books, 1981), 876. Williams's study is an exhaustive and definitive work on Long's life and career; I have relied on it for the facts in this brief discussion of Long's methods and accomplishments.

36. Ibid., 836.

37. Ibid., 545, especially on Long's rapid and decisive tactics to save a Lafayette bank.

38. Ibid., 857. Long did not develop a welfare system in Louisiana, calling it impossible in a traditional agrarian system.

39. Ibid., 761–62.

40. Ibid., 746. Long once ran an oil tax bill through the Louisiana state legislature in about ten minutes to the astonishment of the Standard Oil Company and journalists from all over the country.

41. Ibid., 751.

42. Robert C. Tucker, ed., *The Lenin Anthology* (New York: W. W. Norton and Co., 1975), 550.

43. Ibid., 575.

44. Ibid., 569.

45. Ibid., 574.

46. Maurice Merleau-Ponty, *Humanism and Terror*, trans. John O'Neill (Boston: Beacon Press, 1969), 18.

47. Aristotle, *Nicomachean Ethics*, 6, 7, any edition. For development of this theme, see James V. Schall, *Reason, Revelation, and the Foundations of Political Philosophy* (Baton Rouge: Louisiana State University Press, 1987), 16–62, especially 37: "politics, by limiting itself to what it legitimately is, fulfills its own purposes and protects what is not itself."

48. For development of the theme that politics is the moderate solution to reconciling differences, see my book, *The Activity of Politics and Related Essays* (Selsingrove, Penn.: Susquehanna University Press, 1989), especially 15–25.

49. For development of this theme (without irony), see B. F. Skinner, *Beyond Freedom and Dignity* (New York: Bantam-Vintage Books, 1972).

CHAPTER 2. GEORGE WASHINGTON AND ALEXANDER HAMILTON

1. Quoted in Gerald Stourzh, *Alexander Hamilton and the Idea of Republican Government* (Stanford, Calif.: Stanford University Press, 1970), 201. For a more balanced account of Hamilton as the greater man, see Harvey Flaumenhaft, *The Effective Republic: Administration and Constitution in the Thought of Alexander Hamilton* (Durham, N.C. and London: Duke University Press, 1992), especially, 7–11. Yet I am unable to follow this view, not even on grounds of raw intellectual ability, as it relates to matters of political judgment (except on matters of economic policy where Hamilton had no known peers among the founding generation). The reader interested in making a judgment on this score might start with a detailed reading of Washington's lengthy, paragraph-by-paragraph critique of

James Monroe's criticism of federalist foreign policy toward France: "Remarks on Monroe's 'View of the Conduct of the Executive of the United States,'" in John C. Fitzpatrick, ed., *The Writings of George Washington*, vol. 36 (Washington D.C.: U.S.G.P.O., 1941), 194–237. Consider also in connection with the issue of political judgment, Hamilton's lengthy public criticism of John Adams and its deleterious effects on the political influence of the federalists: "Letter from Alexander Hamilton, Concerning the Public Conduct and Character of John Adams, Esq. President of the United States," in Harold C. Syrett, ed., *The Papers of Alexander Hamilton*, vol. 25 (New York: Columbia University Press, 1977), 169–86. For a sympathetic and insightful account of Hamilton's dependence on the greatness of Washington, see two books by Noemie Emery, *Washington: A Biography* (New York: G. P. Putnam's Sons, 1976), and *Alexander Hamilton: An Intimate Portrait* (New York: G. P. Putnam's Sons, 1982).

2. For example, Hamilton's "Christian Constitutional Societies." See Stourzh, *Alexander Hamilton and the Idea of Republican Government*, 125.

3. The poet Gertrude Stein made Washington's ability to "link this with that" one of the themes in her play *George Washington* (1947); cited in Richard Loss, "The Political Thought of President George Washington," *Presidential Studies Quarterly*, 19, no. 3 (Summer 1989) 485. For a quick appreciation of the respect for the greatness of Washington's vision shown worldwide upon his death, see the tributes collected in the "introduction" to Henry Cabot Lodge, *George Washington* (Boston: Houghton, Mifflin and Co., 1890), especially the report of Talleyrand to Napoleon Bonaparte.

4. W. B. Allen, ed., *George Washington: A Collection* (Indianapolis: Liberty Classics, 1988), 240.

5. Ibid., 240–41.

6. Ibid., 242–43.

7. Ibid., 244.

8. Ibid., 249.

9. Ibid., 398; emphasis added.

10. Ibid., 461; emphasis added.

11. Ibid., 521; emphasis added.

12. For development of this idea, see Loss, "Political Thought," 483.

13. Allen, *George Washington*, 509.

14. To see this criticism articulated in summary form, see Loss, "Political Thought" 482–83. In my view much of this criticism comes from neo-Aristotelians who have not read Cicero's *De Officiis* and its arguments for property rights as the basis for *res publica*. I return to this theme at the end of this chapter.

15. On the other hand, I do not mean to imply that Washington was a political philosopher or a prophet. His writings do not reveal even an implicit understanding of the tensions between Christianity and politics discussed in this book's first chapter, nor does Washington appear to have foreseen as well as Jefferson the tension between "enlightenment science" and politics. I am merely attempting to make the case for the statesmanlike quality of Washington's sustained outlook, that is, one directed toward solutions in the realms of political and military action for the crises and opportunities which came to meet him and his countrymen and women at a particular historical moment.

16. To see this case articulated, see, for example, Glenn A. Phelps, "George Washington and the Paradox of Party," *Presidential Studies Quarterly*, 19, no. 4 (Summer 1989) 733–45.

17. For a lucid and extremely competent account of Hamilton's economic policies in these terms, see Forrest McDonald, *The Presidency of George Washington* (Lawrence, Kans.: University Press of Kansas, 1974), 47–88.

18. Even Hamilton's leanings toward limited Britishlike monarchy derived from the belief that this system was more likely than unfettered democracy to preserve individual liberty. For a balanced and appreciative treatment of Hamilton's political ideas, see Stourzh, *Alexander Hamilton and the Idea of Republican Government*. On the issue of Hamilton's republicanism, see Karl Walling, "America's Machiavellian Moment Reconsidered: War, Liberty, and Virtue in the Commercial Republicanism of Alexander Hamilton," unpublished paper delivered to the 1993 American Political Science Association Meeting, Washington, D.C., especially p. 7: "The rights which Hamilton meant to vindicate required independence. In turn, independence required a people with the spirit to assert their liberty, and the means to defend it against all enemies, foreign and domestic. While Jefferson looked to the frontier as the means to preserve the spirit of a free people, Hamilton looked to commerce and effective government. . . . Hamilton laid the foundations of the commercial republic which is now the source of America's remarkable ability to wage war without losing its liberty in the process." To Walling's remarks I would add two qualifications: Hamilton *aided* Washington in laying the foundations of such a republic, and "America's remarkable ability to wage war without losing its liberty in this process" should be amended to say "heretofore." On this latter issue, see 111–12 of my essay "American Democracy and the Punitive Use of Force," in Wendell J. Coats, Jr., ed., *A Theory of Republican Character and Related Essays* (London and Toronto: Associated University Press, 1994).

19. For an account of Hamilton's last few years, see Douglass Adair and Marvin Harvey, "Was Alexander Hamilton a Christian Statesman?" *William and Mary Quarterly*, 12 (April 1955), 308–29. See also on the changes in Hamilton after Washington's death, Emery, *Alexander Hamilton*, 245–59.

20. For development of this theme, see Stourzh, *Alexander Hamilton and the Idea of Republican Government*, especially 171–205.

21. See the introduction to *The Living Thoughts of Thomas Jefferson*, ed. John Dewey (New York: Longman, Green and Co., 1940), 1–29.

22. Dewey, *Living Thoughts of Thomas Jefferson*, 66.

23. Quoted in Edward Mead Earle, ed., *Makers of Modern Strategy* (Princeton: Princeton University Press, 1971), 138.

24. For development of this theme, see McDonald, *The Presidency of George Washington*, 47–88.

25. See Stourzh, *Alexander Hamilton and the Idea of Republican Government*, for exploration of the philosophic sources of Hamilton's thought.

26. For development of this idea, see Richard Ellis and Aaron Wildavsky, "'Greatness' Revisited: Evaluating the Performance of Early American Presidents in Terms of Cultural Dilemmas," *Presidential Studies Quarterly*, 21, no. 1 (Winter, 1991), 21–22.

27. This is the way in which Adair and Harvey treat Hamilton's attempts to deal with the various ethical contradictions that he faced in "Was Alexander Hamilton a Christian Statesman?"

28. Washington recommended that a single volume of Cicero's writings be prepared for use in the nation's schools.

29. "For . . . it is the peculiar function of the state and the city to guarantee to everyman the free and undisturbed control of his own particular property. . . .

For the chief purpose in the establishment of the constitutional state . . . was that individual property rights might be secured." Cicero, *De Officiis* 2, 21–22, trans. Walter Miller (Cambridge: Harvard University Press, 1913), Loeb Classical Library, 249, 255.

30. Obviously even foundings can be considered partisan in the broadest sense, because the institutions they establish all embody some particular conception of a just order. However, on this logic, constitutions that "mix" the influence of various classes and interests may be considered less "partisan" than others.

Chapter 3. Abraham Lincoln

1. For a critical discussion by a political theorist of some of the themes in the historical literature, especially the modern view that Lincoln forced an "illusory alternative" on the country, see Harry V. Jaffa, *Crisis of the House Divided: An Interpretation of the Issues in the Lincoln-Douglas Debates*, Phoenix edition (Chicago: University of Chicago Press, 1982), 7–37.

2. For a discussion of Lincoln's oratorical powers, see Lord Charnwood, *Abraham Lincoln*, 2d ed. (New York: Henry Holt & Co., 1917), 122–37.

3. Quoted in Jaffa, *Crisis of the House Divided*, 189.

4. *The Lincoln Encyclopedia* (hereafter, *TLE*), ed. Archer H. Shaw (New York: MacMillan Company, 1950), 10.

5. Ibid., 384.

6. Ibid., 45.

7. Ibid., 75.

8. Ibid., 10.

9. Ibid., 41.

10. Ibid., 41.

11. This is not merely a theoretical issue, because upon it turns the question of whether Lincoln would have, if able, led the nation into a civil war merely to realize what he perceived to be his cosmic destiny. I am suggesting that the question is unanswerable because it involves *making explicit* distinctions of which Lincoln left no evidence. Nor can reductionist psychological modes of explanation shed light here because they treat both political and transpolitical ideas as merely epiphenomena of a process of personal "adjustment."

12. Quoted in Jaffa, *Crisis of the House Divided*, 331.

13. Ibid.

14. Shaw, *TLE*, 109.

15. Ibid., 261.

16. Ibid., 180.

17. Ibid., 113.

18. For development of this point, see Jaffa, *Crisis of the House Divided*, 318–27.

19. For more on this, see the entries under "Labor, Relationship of, and Capital," in Shaw, *TLE*, 180–81.

20. Ibid., 325.

21. Ibid., 325.

22. Ibid., 69.

23. See Lincoln's repeated assertions collected by Shaw, in *TLE*, under the entry, "Slavery, Conspiracy to Promote," 302–5.

24. Jaffa, *Crisis of the House Divided*, 402–3.

25. Shaw, *TLE*, 63.

26. Ibid., 289.

27. Ibid., 41.

28. Ibid., 226.

29. Ibid.

30. Ibid., 52–54.

31. Ibid., 228; emphasis added.

32. For development of these points, see Jaffa, *Crisis of the House Divided*, Appendix I ("Some of the Historical Background to the Lincoln-Douglas Debates") and Appendix II ("Some Notes on the Dred Scott Decision"), 430–44.

33. Shaw, *TLE*, 26.

34. See the critical discussion by Jaffa of the 1929 essay by Charles W. Ramsdell on the "natural limits to slavery" in *Crisis of the House Divided*, 385–99.

35. Alfred H. Conrad and John Meyer, "The Economics of Slavery in the Ante-Bellum South," *Journal of Political Economy* (April 1958), cited in Jaffa, *Crisis of the House Divided*, 396.

36. Shaw, *TLE*, 36.

37. Jaffa, *Crisis of the House Divided*, 190.

38. This was a decision of not only immediate military significance but of strategic or political as well, because it essentially "undid" the social structure the South was fighting to preserve.

39. James Fenimore Cooper, *The American Democrat* (New York: Alfred A. Knopf, 1931), 13–15.

40. For a discussion of the differences between a substantive goal and a general goal and the difficulties in trying to make the former the basis for civil association, see Michael J. Oakeshott, *On Human Conduct* (Oxford: Clarendon Press, 1975), 119.

41. "Lincoln accomplished this . . . by assigning to the federal power a general responsibility for the well-being of American citizens. This much it accomplished by freeing the slaves and preserving the Union by military means—not by persuasion and politics—thus putting the civil bond which makes a nation on a new basis." M. E. Bradford, "From the Family of the Lion" (review of James M. McPherson, *Abraham Lincoln and the Second American Revolution*), in *Chronicles*, December 1991, 31.

42. Alexis de Tocqueville, *Democracy in America*, vol. 2, Book 2, chap. 1, any edition.

43. Harry Jaffa has suggested four general criteria for judging cases of statesmanship: "Is the goal a worthy one; second, does the statesman judge wisely as to what is and what is not within his power; third are the means selected apt to produce the intended results; and, fourth . . . does he say or do anything to hinder future statesmen from more perfectly attaining his goal when altered conditions bring more of that goal within range of possibility?" *Crisis of the House Divided*, 370.

44. Shaw, *TLE*, 40.

45. For development of this theme, see C. G. Jung, *Psychology and Religion* (New Haven: Yale University Press, 1938), 58–61.

46. Jaffa, *Crisis of the House Divided*, 238–39.

47. For development of the theme about constitutional crises and statesmanship, see Morton J. Frisch and Richard G. Stevens, *American Political Thought: The Philosophic Dimension of American Statesmanship* (New York: Charles Scribner's Sons, 1971), 3–21.

48. By historian David M. Potter; quoted in James M. McPherson, *Abraham*

Lincoln and the Second American Revolution (New York: Oxford University Press, 1991), 93. In addition to McPherson, see also on Lincoln's use of language as a form of influence, Jacques Barzun, *Lincoln, the Literary Genius* (Evanston, Ill.: Evanston Publishing Co., 1960).

49. For a lucid and competent summary account of Lincoln as war leader, see McPherson, *Abraham Lincoln and the Second American Revolution*, chapter 4, "Lincoln and the Strategy of Unconditional Surrender," 65–112.

50. See, for an introduction to this subject, Ernest Lee Tuveson, *Redeemer Nation: The Idea of America's Millennial Role* (Chicago: University of Chicago Press, 1968); see also, Eric Voegelin, *The New Science of Politics* (Chicago: University of Chicago Press, 1952).

51. Again it is difficult to know exactly how to classify Lincoln on the issue of millennialism. Consider, for example, the following statement: "Human nature. . . is God's decree and can never be reversed" (Shaw, *TLE*, 152). This hardly sounds like the sentiment of a millennialist reformer.

CHAPTER 4. WOODROW WILSON

1. For a detailed discussion of Wilson as a legislative leader, see Kendrik A. Clements, *The Presidency of Woodrow Wilson* (Lawrence: University Press of Kansas, 1992), 31–92.

2. Joseph Cropsey, "The United States as Regime and the Sources of the American Way of Life," in *The Moral Foundations of the American Republic*, ed. Robert H. Horwitz (Charlottesville: University Press of Virginia, 1986), 180.

3. Woodrow Wilson, "The Study of Administration," in *The Papers of Woodrow Wilson*, ed. Arthur S. Link, vol. 5, 1885–88, (Princeton: Princeton University Press, 1968), 369.

4. Quoted in Paul Eidelberg, *A Discourse on Statesmanship: The Design and Transformation of the American Polity* (Urbana: University of Illinois Press, 1974), 286–87.

5. Quoted in E. David Cronon, ed., *The Political Thought of Woodrow Wilson* (Indianapolis: The Boobs-Merrill Company, Inc., 1965), 525.

6. Quoted in Eidelberg, *Discourse on Statesmanship*, 359.

7. Quoted in Clements, *Presidency of Woodrow Wilson*, 7–8.

8. Eidelberg, *Discourse on Statesmanship*, 358.

9. Quoted in Eidelberg, *Discourse on Statesmanship*, 315–16.

10. Ibid., 279.

11. Ibid., 348.

12. For a discussion of these developments, starting with the *Slaughterhouse* ruling, see James M. McPherson, *Abraham Lincoln and the Second American Revolution* (New York: Oxford University Press, 1991), 145–52.

13. Eidelberg, *Discourse on Statesmanship*, 279.

14. See, for a discussion, Clements, *Presidency of Woodrow Wilson*, 9–10.

15. Quoted in Eidelberg, *Discourse on Statesmanship*, 292.

16. Ibid., 334.

17. Ibid., 335.

18. Eidelberg, *Discourse on Statesmanship*, 336.

19. Quoted in Eidelberg, *Discourse on Statesmanship*, 343.

20. Eidelberg, *Discourse on Statesmanship*, 342.

21. Ibid., 363. To see this contrast extended into the realm of foreign policy, see Henry Kissinger, *Diplomacy* (New York: Simon and Schuster, 1994), 29–35.

22. Eidelberg, *Discourse on Statesmanship,* 347.

23. Quoted in Eidelberg, *Discourse on Statesmanship,* 346.

24. Ernest Lee Tuveson, *Redeemer Nation: The Idea of America's Millennial Role* (Chicago: The University of Chicago Press, 1968), 34.

25. Ibid., 127.

26. Ibid., 209–13, provides relevant excerpts.

27. Clements, *Presidency of Woodrow Wilson,* 1–2.

28. Woodrow Wilson, "Address to Confederate Veterans at Washington, June 5, 1917," in *The Public Papers of Woodrow Wilson,* eds. Ray Stannard Baker and William E. Dodd, vol. 5 (New York: Harper & Brothers, 1927), 55. This passage by Wilson is remarkable for the simplemindedness of the argument that although providence was mysterious, and although we could not read its purposes during the Civil War, these purposes were now open to us a mere half-century later. St. Augustine, for one, must have been turning in his grave. This Wilsonian exercise in theodicy exceeds, in its "certainty," even Lincoln's thought that since God could have stopped the war, and had not, therefore He must will that it continue.

29. Quoted in August Heckscher, ed., *The Politics of Woodrow Wilson* (New York: Harper & Brothers, 1956), 105.

30. Ibid., 385.

31. Richard J. Bishirjian, "Croly, Wilson, and the American Civil Religion," *Modern Age,* vol. 23 (Winter 1979) 37.

32. Quoted in Heckscher, *Politics of Woodrow Wilson,* 338.

33. See on this subject Heckscher, *Politics of Woodrow Wilson,* 78–106.

34. Eidelberg, *Discourse on Statesmanship,* 329–30.

35. See on this subject Wilson's address to the McCormick Theological Seminary in 1909, reproduced in Heckscher, *Politics of Woodrow Wilson,* 78–83, especially 78: "The end and object of Christianity is the individual, and the individual is the vehicle of Christianity. . . . no organization is in any proper sense Christian."

36. Quoted in Cronon, *Political Thought of Woodrow Wilson,* 420.

37. Quoted in Heckscher, *Politics of Woodrow Wilson,* 385.

38. Quoted in Clements, *Presidency of Woodrow Wilson,* 223.

39. Bishirjian, "Croly, Wilson, and the American Civil Religion," 38.

40. On the "closeness" of the 1912 election (in spite of Wilson's electoral vote tally), see Clements, *Presidency of Woodrow Wilson,* 29.

41. See the quotation from Lincoln reproduced in the chapter on Lincoln in this book, 57.

42. My point is that the consequences of Wilson's hostility to formalism and his *immanentist* civil religion both reflect worrisome tendencies which Tocqueville warned America to avoid if it wished to keep its democracy healthy. Respect for forms and formality and appreciation of *transcendent* realities serve as counterweights to the embalanced democratic tendency toward physical and material gratification. For development of this latter theme, see the title essay of my book, *A Theory of Republican Character and Related Essays;* for a sketch of the characteristics of a politics of civility, see the title essay of my book, *The Activity of Politics and Related Essays.*

CHAPTER 5. WINSTON CHURCHILL

1. In addition to serving as a cavalry officer in his youth and wartime leader of Britain in his later years, Churchill also held the following offices in the first

three decades of the twentieth century: undersecretary of state for colonies, president of the board of trade, home secretary, first lord of the Admiralty (1911–15), minister of munitions, secretary of state for war and air, and secretary of state for colonies. Martin Gilbert, *Churchill's Political Philosophy* (New York: Oxford University Press, 1981), 37, n. 1. See, also Gilbert, *Churchill: A Life* (New York: Henry Holt and Co., 1991), 51–489.

2. Gilbert, *Churchill's Political Philosophy*, 10.

3. Winston Churchill, *The Second World War*, vol. 1 of *The Gathering Storm* (Boston: Houghton-Mifflin Co., 1985), xvi.

4. Churchill, *Second World War*, 16–17.

5. Ibid., 6.

6. Ibid., 6.

7. Ibid., 8–9.

8. Ibid., 23.

9. Ibid., 12.

10. Ibid., 39.

11. Ibid., 13.

12. Ibid., 9.

13. See, for Churchill's account of German rearmament, ibid., 35–214.

14. Ibid., 46.

15. See especially, Jeffrey D. Wallin, "Politics and Strategy in the Dardanelles Operations," *Statesmanship: Essays in Honor of Sir Winston Churchill*, ed. in Harry Jaffa (Durham, N.C.: Carolina Academic Press, 1981), 131–55; also, Gilbert, *Churchill: A Life*, 288–307.

16. For explicit discussion of this point, see the introductory essay to *The Gathering Storm*, by John Keegan, especially p. x: "Like Clarendon and Macaulay, he saw history as a branch of moral philosophy."

17. Quoted in Gilbert, *Churchill: A Life*, 188.

18. Quoted in Kirk Emmert, "Winston S. Churchill on Civilizing Empire," in *Statesmanship: Essays in Honor of Sir Winston Churchill*, ed. Harry Jaffa (Durham, N.C.: Carolina Academic Press, 1981), 63.

19. For a discussion, see Wayne C. Thompson, "Winston S. Churchill: States- man as Strategist," in *Statesmanship: Essays in Honor of Sir Winston Churchill*, ed. Harry Jaffa (Durham, N.C.: Carolina Academic Press, 1981), 121–24.

20. This is a major theme of von Clausewitz's classic work, *On War*. See espe- cially, Book 1, chap. 1, Section 11, in any edition.

21. James M. McPerson, *Abraham Lincoln and the Second American Revolution* (New York: Oxford University Press, 1991), 65–112.

22. On this point here is an interesting comment from General Dwight Eisen- hower in 1943: "I am so incredibly naive that I do not realize that the Britishers instinctively approach every military problem from the viewpoint of the Em- pire." Cited in Warren F. Kimball, *The Juggler: Franklin Roosevelt as Wartime States- man* (Princeton: Princeton University Press, 1991), 66.

23. "The distinction between politics and strategy diminishes as the point of view is raised. At the summit true politics and strategy are one." Quoted in Wallin, "Politics and Strategy," 154.

24. Gordon A. Craig, "The Political Leader as Strategist," in *Makers of Modern Strategy* ed. Peter Paret (Princeton: Princeton University Press, 1986), 503.

25. Lord (General) Ismay said that "in his grasp of strategy," Churchill "stood head and shoulders above his professional advisers." Cited in Craig, "Political Leader as Strategist," 502.

26. "On August 16, 1940, for instance, to the astonishment of Chief of the Imperial General Staff Sir John Dill and Major-General Sir John Kennedy, director of military operations, he sent a directive for the conduct of the campaign in the Middle East that was virtually on operations order, including detailed tactical instructions, down to the forward and rear distribution of battalions, and giving minutely detailed orders for the employment of forces." Craig, "Political Leader as Strategist," 499.

27. Gilbert, *Churchill: A Life*, 96–97.

28. Ibid., 239–307.

29. On this point, see Wallin, "Politics and Strategy," and Craig, "Political Leader as Strategist."

30. Craig, "Political Leader as Strategist," 500.

31. For de Gaulle's views, see Jean Lacouture, *De Gaulle: The Rebel 1890–1944*, trans. by Patrick O'Brian (New York: W. W. Norton and Co., 1990), 268–81.

32. Gilbert, *Churchill's Political Philosophy*, 68.

33. Quoted in Gilbert, *Churchill's Political Philosophy*, 10.

34. Apropos of this aspect of Churchill's character is the reported remark of T. E. Lawrence (Lawrence of Arabia) that Churchill was capable on occasion of "chucking" the statesmanlike course and doing the "honest" thing. (One interpretation of this quip is that when the stakes were not too high, Churchill was willing to act in his public dealings on an individual basis toward those with whom he dealt.)

35. Quoted in Gilbert, *Churchill's Political Philosophy*, 11.

36. Quoted in Harry Jaffa, *Crisis of the House Divided* (Chicago: University of Chicago Press, 1982), 46.

37. Quoted in Gilbert, *Churchill's Political Philosophy*, 42–43.

38. Gilbert, *Churchill's Political Philosophy*, 45–46.

39. Ibid., 50.

40. At the turn of the century, Churchill's remarks occasionally evince the idea of a providential plan for the British empire, but the plan is not millennialist and does not entail the fundamental transformation of human nature—it is simply concerned with the spread of British civilization to the colonial world and especially the principles of British justice. Here is a representative remark from that period of his life (age 22): "We shall continue to pursue that course marked out for us by an all-wise hand and carry out our mission of bearing peace, civilisation and good government to the uttermost ends of the earth." Gilbert, *Churchill: A Life*, 72.

41. Quoted in Gilbert, *Churchill's Political Philosophy*, 7.

42. Ibid., 45–46.

43. Ibid., 46–47.

44. Ibid., 43.

45. For a discussion of the groups and personalities involved, see Steven A. Maaranen, "The Struggle for a New World Order: The Foreign Policy of the British Left, 1932–1939," in *Statesmanship: Essays in Honor of Sir Winston Churchill* ed. Harry Jaffa (Durham: N.C.: Carolina Academic Press, 1981), 157–211.

46. Gilbert, *Churchill's Political Philosophy*, 5.

47. Ibid.

48. Ibid., 82.

49. "Wilson's own philosophy—disarmament, anti-imperialism and a concert for international peace . . . echoed Gladstonianism in a conscious way. . . . both had an intense conviction that . . . their nation stood in the vanguard of God's

design for the future prosperity and welfare of the human race." David Reynold, "Rethinking Anglo-American Relations," *International Affairs*, 65, no. 1 (Winter 1988/89), 102.

50. Lord Birkenhead, one of Churchill's closest friends, wrote of Churchill "that a friend once lent him Welldon's translation of Aristotle's 'Ethics.' . . . Winston read it (or read part of it) and is reported to have said that he thought it very good. 'But,' he added, 'it is extraordinary how much of it I had already thought out for myself.'" Quoted in Emmert, "Winston S. Churchill on Civilizing Empire," 64.

51. Emmert, "Winston S. Churchill on Civilizing Empire," 88.

52. Ibid., 89; emphasis added.

53. Kimball, *The Juggler*, 186; emphasis added.

54. Ibid., 191.

55. One of the recurring themes of Gilbert's *Churchill: A Life* is Churchill's extraordinary personal energy and fear of inactivity. My point in this regard is simply that perpetual confrontation is one way of avoiding "inactivity."

Chapter 6. Charles de Gaulle

1. Jean Lacouture, *De Gaulle: The Ruler, 1945–1970*, trans. Alan Sheridan (New York: W. W. Norton & Co., 1992), 123 and 237.

2. See especially, *Vers L'Armée de Métier* (Paris: Presses Pocket, 1934). For a detailed English summary, see Will Morrisey, *Reflections on De Gaulle: Political Founding in Modernity* (Lanham, Md.: University Press of America, 1983), 47–56.

3. A dramatic example is de Gaulle's "Brazzaville address" of 30 January 1944, which implies the need for the end of colonialism, in *The War Memoirs of Charles de Gaulle: Unity, 1942–1944, Documents* (New York: Simon and Schuster, 1959), 248–51.

4. Here is U.S. Ambassador Robert Murphy's reflection on de Gaulle's prescience: "His thoughts were two jumps ahead of everybody else's. In 1943, de Gaulle had correctly calculated that Allied victory was certain and that France would share in that victory regardless of what France accomplished or failed to do." Cited in Jean Lacouture, *De Gaulle: The Rebel, 1890–1944*, trans. Patrick O'Brian (New York: W. W. Norton & Co., 1990), 429.

5. Here is former President Richard Nixon on de Gaulle's television addresses to the French people: "His delivery was masterly. . . . He used the French language with the same grandeur and eloquence with which Churchill used English. It was a classical, almost archaic French. Yet he spoke so articulately and with such precision that his message seemed to resonate apart from his words." Richard Nixon, *Leaders* (New York: Warner Books, Inc., 1982), 56–57.

6. "Your sensitive souls have undoubtedly read many things by Jean-Jacques Rousseau, but not *Le Contrat social*—which despite its reputation is a powerful book." De Gaulle to André Malraux, cited in André Malraux, *Felled Oaks: Conversation with De Gaulle* (New York: Holt, Rinehart and Winston, 1972), 100–101.

7. See Malraux, *Felled Oaks*, especially 28.

8. See n. 50 below.

9. Malraux, *Felled Oaks*, 25.

10. Charles de Gaulle, *War Memoirs: The Call to Honour, 1940–1942*, Documents (New York: The Viking Press, 1955), 11–12.

11. Cited in Lacouture, *De Gaulle: The Ruler*, 365.

12. Malraux, *Felled Oaks*, 17–18; emphasis added.

13. Lacouture, *De Gaulle: The Rebel*, 436–37.

14. Charles de Gaulle, *The Edge of the Sword*, trans. Gerald Hopkins (New York: Criterion Books, 1960), 106.

15. Ibid., 126–27.

16. See, in this connection, Richard Nixon, *In the Arena: A Memoir of Victory, Defeat, and Renewal* (New York: Simon and Schuster, 1990), 272.

17. Charles de Gaulle, *Memoirs of Hope: Renewal and Endeavor* (New York: Simon and Schuster, 1971), 133.

18. The French economic plan is "indicative," setting medium term goals and creating financial inducements to make them attractive to investors. For a detailed discussion in English of the inception of French planning, see Andrew Shonfield, *Modern Capitalism: The Changing Balance of Public and Private Power* (London: Oxford University Press, 1969), 121–50.

19. De Gaulle, *Memoirs of Hope*, 134.

20. Ibid., 135.

21. Paul Johnson, *Modern Times: The World from the Twenties to the Eighties* (New York: Harper & Row, 1983), 596; emphasis added.

22. Ibid., 595.

23. Aristotle made a similar observation twenty-four hundred years earlier. See *The Politics*, Book 7, Ch. 7, any edition.

24. *The War Memoirs of Charles de Gaulle: Salvation, 1944–1946, Documents* (New York: Simon and Schuster, 1960), 387. For a general description of the political arrangements of the Fourth French Republic, see Stanley Hoffmann, "The Institutions of the Fifth Republic," in *Searching for the New France*, eds. James Hollifield and George Ross (New York: Routledge, 1991), 43–44.

25. *War Memoirs of Charles de Gaulle: Salvation, 1944–46, Documents*, 387.

26. Ibid., 389.

27. Ibid., 390.

28. Hoffmann, "Institutions of the Fifth Republic," 53–54; emphasis added.

29. In this connection, see chap. 1, n. 27 of this book.

30. See Johnson, *Modern Times*, 502.

31. See Lacouture, *De Gaulle: The Ruler*, 176.

32. See Johnson, *Modern Times*, 504–5.

33. Ibid., 504. For a critical treatment of de Gaulle's handling of the Algerian crisis from the standpoint of its implications for patriotism, see Angelo Codevilla, "De Gaulle: Statesmanship in the Modern State," in *Statesmanship: Essays in Honor of Sir Winston Churchill*, ed. Harry Jaffa (Durham, N.C.: Carolina Academic Press, 1981), 226–27.

34. See Johnson, *Modern Times*, 503, for this assessment.

35. Lacouture, *De Gaulle: The Rebel*, 335.

36. De Gaulle, *The Edge of the Sword*, 9.

37. Quoted in Jean Monnet, *Memoirs*, trans. Richard Mayne (Garden City, N.Y.: Doubleday, 1978), 441.

38. "In short, General de Gaulle was a 'European' much more by school, book, and museum, than by systems and treaties. He believed that poets were greater unifiers than ideologues, artists and soldiers more creative of convergences than technocrats. He believed Chekhov and Bartok to be greater than Jean Monnet— and perhaps even Karl Marx." Lacouture, *De Gaulle: The Ruler*, 398.

39. Monnet, *Memoirs*, 443–44.

40. Ibid., 487; emphasis added.

41. Ibid., 524; emphasis added.

42. De Gaulle, *The Edge of the Sword*, 15.

43. "In so highly symbolic a character, how can one distinguish between a will for power and an awareness of incarnation? This insistence upon thrusting his rival aside can be seen as the expression of a feeling for the nation just as well as an eagerness to rule." Lacouture, *De Gaulle: The Rebel*, 436.

44. Quoted in Lacouture, *De Gaulle: The Rebel*, 13.

45. Ibid., 245; emphasis added.

46. Ibid., 127; emphasis added.

47. "No historian has attempted to analyze the most curious element in history: the moment at which *the current begins to flow*. For us or against us. . . . It does not flow by chance, I am sure. Still, what makes it flow is never decisive. Sometimes it disappears as rapidly as it has come. . . . I'm speaking of what gives soul to a people—or to an army." De Gaulle to Malraux, quoted in Malraux, *Felled Oaks*, 108–9. This is a curious statement for one as well read as de Gaulle, for this is clearly one of the central themes of Machiavelli's discourses on Livy and the Roman republic.

48. Quoted in Johnson, *Modern Times*, 595.

49. Quoted in Malraux, *Felled Oaks*, 124.

50. Ibid., 123.

51. Ibid., 109.

52. On this theme see Lacouture, *De Gaulle: The Ruler*, 469. Here is Nixon's assessment of de Gaulle's unique achievements: "These conclusions are clear: Without de Gaulle, France might not have survived the tragedy of defeat in World War II. Without de Gaulle, France might not have recovered from the devastation of World War II. Without de Gaulle, the Franco-German rapprochement might not have been achieved. Without de Gaulle, France would not have adopted the constitution of the Fifth Republic and might have sunk into chaos politically, economically, and socially. And without de Gaulle, the spirit of France . . . might have died instead of being as vital and strong as it is today." Richard Nixon, *Leaders*, 80. For a more critical view of de Gaulle's achievements as lowering the standards of statesmanship from glory (de Gaulle never appeared to believe that virtue was a possible political end) to the granting of economic advantages, see Codevilla, "De Gaulle: Statesmanship in the Modern State," 232–33. The quotations I have selected from Malraux's interview with de Gaulle (*Felled Oaks*) would suggest that de Gaulle would agree with this assessment. The issue for our analysis is whether the granting of economic benefits as the primary task of leaders can any longer be considered statesmanship, that is, require a political vocabulary to describe what it is doing.

53. De Gaulle's words in a 1960 address at Westminster are revealing in this regard: "With self-assurance, without being aware of it, you operate in a secure, stable political system. So strong are your traditions and loyalties in the political field that your government is quite naturally endowed with cohesion and permanence. . . . I can tell you that this England, which keeps itself in order while practising respect for the liberties of all, inspires trust in France." Quoted in Lacouture, *De Gaulle: The Ruler*, 352.

54. Quoted in Lacouture, *De Gaulle: The Ruler*, 163.

55. Quoted in Malraux, *Felled Oaks*, 114; emphasis added.

56. See in this connection, chap. 1, n. 47, of this book.

57. Lacouture, *De Gaulle: The Ruler*, 7–8.

58. For explicit development of this theme, see Will Morrisey's analysis of de Gaulle's 1924 book, *La Discorde Chez L'Ennemi*, in *Reflections on De Gaulle*, 3–22.

CHAPTER 7. RICHARD NIXON AND HENRY KISSINGER

1. On Nixon and Kissinger as a team, here is Nixon himself: "The combination was unlikely—the grocer's son from Whittier and the refugee from Hitler's Germany, the politician and the academic. But our differences helped make the partnership work." Richard Nixon, *The Memoirs of Richard Nixon* (New York: Grosset & Dunlap, 1978), 341. For a more cynical view, see Walter Isaacson, *Kissinger: A Biography* (New York: Simon & Schuster, 1992), 139–44. For the view that the grand strategic aims of Nixon and Kissinger were at odds, with Kissinger favoring the "eastern establishment" view for a "new global order" (e.g., U.S. withdrawal from Vietnam) and Nixon a modified containment strategy (e.g., a permanent U.S. presence in South Vietnam), see Richard Thornton, *The Nixon Kissinger Years: Reshaping America's Foreign Policy* (New York: Paragon House, 1989). It is difficult to know what to make of Thornton's thesis, which differentiates sharply between the two over the entire time Nixon was in office. Thornton even suggests that Kissinger was actually in charge of American foreign policy from Winter 1972 until the end of the Ford administration. At this point in the historical record, it does not seem possible to evaluate the accuracy of Thornton's thesis, especially where it is contradicted by the accounts of the participants themselves. For a case in point, contrast the accounts of the 1972 "Christmas bombing" in the memoirs of Nixon and of Kissinger with the account in Thornton, 170–74.

2. See, in particular, Richard Nixon, *Leaders* (New York: Warner Books, 1982), especially chap. 9, "In the Arena: Reflections on Leadership," 320–45. For Kissinger see especially Henry Kissinger, *White House Years* (Boston: Little, Brown and Company, 1979), chap. 3, "Convictions of an Apprentice Statesman," 54–70; Henry Kissinger, "The White Revolutionary: Reflections on Bismarck," *Daedalus*, 97 (Summer 1968), 888–923; and Henry Kissinger, *Diplomacy* (New York: Simon and Schuster, 1994).

3. Paul Johnson, "In Praise of Richard Nixon," *Commentary* 86, no. 4 (October 1988), 50–53. For a brief but balanced view putting Kissinger in perspective, see Josef Joffe, "In Defense of Henry Kissinger," *Commentary*, 96, no. 6 (December 1992), 49–52. Joffe's essay is a reply to the high-minded cynicism of the Isaacson book cited in n. 1 above.

4. For reasoned speculation about Kant's influence on Kissinger's outlook, see Peter W. Dickson, *Kissinger and the Meaning of History* (Cambridge: Cambridge University Press, 1978).

5. For Kissinger's criticism of Kant for inconsistency on the meanings of the historical and the transcendental, see Gregory D. Cleva, *Henry Kissinger and the American Approach to Foreign Policy* (London and Toronto: Associated University Presses, 1989), which cites on 36 these sentences in criticism of Kant from Kissinger's Harvard undergraduate honors thesis: "The realm of freedom and necessity cannot be reconciled except by an inward experience. The mechanism of nature offers no obvious assurance for the implementation of freedom." Whatever else Kissinger may not be called a millennialist.

6. On this, see Thornton, *Nixon-Kissinger Years*, 170.

7. On the evolution of the meaning of "arms control," see Lawrence Freed-

man, *The Evolution of Nuclear Strategy* (New York: St. Martin's Press, 1983), 190–207.

8. For expanded treatment of this theme, see my article, "The Ideology of Arms Control," *Journal of Contemporary Studies*, 5, no. 3 (Summer 1982), 3–15; reprinted in Wendell J. Coats, Jr., *The Activity of Politics and Related Essays* (London and Toronto: Associated University Presses, 1989), 58–71.

9. For an extremely critical view of the Reagan administration on "arms control," see Malcolm Wallop and Angelo Codevilla, *The Arms Control Delusion* (San Francisco: ICS Press, 1987), 134–73.

10. Speech delivered in Brussel on 1 September 1979 and printed in *Survival* 21, no. 6 (November–December 1979), 264–68, under the title, "NATO: The Next Thirty Years by Henry A. Kissinger"; this quotation is from 265.

11. It was, of course, never explicitly acknowledged as such.

12. For development of this theme, see my article cited in n. 8 above. See also Wendell J. Coats, Jr., "The Malingering McNamara Model for the Use of U.S. Military Force," *Strategic Review*, 17, no. 4 (Fall 1989), 18–30.

13. On the relative significance and insignificance of the "Watergate scandal," I follow Paul Johnson's account, *Modern Times: The World from the Twenties to the Nineties*, rev. ed. (New York: Harper Collins Publishers, 1991), 650–54. For a considerably different view, see Stephen E. Ambrose, *Nixon: Ruin and Recovery, 1973–1990* (New York: Simon & Schuster, 1991). See also, Richard E. Neustadt, *Presidental Power and the Modern Presidents* (New York: The Free Press, 1990), 212–14.

14. Henry Kissinger, *Years of Upheaval* (Boston: Little, Brown and Company, 1982), 260.

15. The Pentagon had already decided to dismantle the Safeguard system at Grand Forks, North Dakota, in July 1976. See "Senate Approves Defense Spending of $90.7 Billion," *New York Times*, 19 November 1975, 1 and 12.

16. Kissinger, *Years of Upheaval*, 1194.

17. For a lengthy discussion of the technical issues, see Ernest J. Yanarella, *The Missile Defense Controversy* (Lexington: University of Kentucky Press, 1977).

18. See, for example, Wallop and Codevilla, *Arms Control Delusion*, 95–96. One outspoken opponent at the time was Senator Robert Dole.

19. See n. 10 above; see also Kissinger, *Years of Upheaval*, 257–58.

20. Nixon, *Memoirs of Richard Nixon*, 551 and 617–18.

21. Interesting in this context is Kissinger's assessment of Bismarck's view of the source of limits in international power relations: "Bismarck believed that a correct evaluation of power would yield a doctrine of self-limitation; the conservatives insisted that force could be restrained only by superior principle." Kissinger, "White Revolutionary," 914. Was Kissinger trying to follow Bismarck here? If so, did he make "a correct evaluation of power"? For his latest views on the ABM incident, see Kissinger, *Diplomacy*, 751.

22. For development of this theme, see Isaacson, *Kissinger: A Biography*.

23. See n. 8 above.

24. For development of this theme, see the book by Kissinger's then Harvard colleague, Tom Schelling, *Arms and Influence* (New Haven: Yale University Press, 1966). On Kissinger's admitted respect for Schelling's ideas, see Cleva, *Henry Kissinger and the American Approach*, 120. But see also Isaacson, *Kissinger: A Biography*, 280–81.

25. Samuel P. Huntington, *The Soldier and the State* (Cambridge, Mass.: Harvard University Press 1957), 465–66.

26. For explorations of this general theme written during the events in question, see Raymond Aron, *The Imperial Republic: The United States and the World, 1945–1973,* trans. Frank Jellinek (Cambridge, Mass.: Winthrop Publishers, 1974), 252–329; and Robert W. Tucker, *Nation or Empire? The Debate over American Foreign Policy* (Baltimore, Md.: Johns Hopkins Press, 1968), 134–60. Tucker tentatively concludes that an "imperial policy might well lead in time to the derangement of our political institutions, but Vietnam has not had this effect," because it has led (in 1968) to greater Senate independence in foreign policy (134). Neither of these books addresses the specific considerations I am raising here.

27. The literature here is abundant, but for a particularly candid and emotional statement, see (LTC) F. Charles Parker IV, *Vietnam: Strategy for a Stalemate* (New York: Paragon House, 1989), 236. Parker's book provides useful new information on Soviet geopolitical aims (vis-à-vis the United States and China) in supporting North Vietnam. The book's shortcoming, in my view, is not to associate the failure or refusal of the Johnson administration to act on such considerations with the influence of a dominant intellectual paradigm for "national security," which was to make us autonomous of all old ("unstable") balance of power considerations through "existential" or "finite" deterrence at the nuclear level and through "economically rational" use of force at nonnuclear levels.

28. That is, by logical implication that the military craft no longer had autonomy over its own internal, tactical skills.

29. The literature here is also abundant, but for a recent account that takes its bearings explicitly from (the present irrelevance of) Huntington's thesis, see A. J. Bacevich, "Gays and the Military Culture," *National Review,* XLV, no. 8 (26 April 1993), 26–31.

30. Both Nixon and Kissinger were keen on the idea of bold, imaginative, and "creative" actions during major crises as a way to restructure relations among nations. In my view this approach occasionally blurred into political Romanticism and plain bad judgment. For a case in point, see Kissinger's bizarre praise of Anwar Sadat for initiating the 1973 war with Israel in order to break up a stalemated, negotiating situation. *Years of Upheaval,* 460.

31. Henry Kissinger, *Nuclear Weapons and Foreign Policy* (New York: Harper & Brothers, 1957), 141.

32. Thornton, *Nixon-Kissinger Years,* 357. Still no doubt Nixon would have tried harder if he had had effective power after 1972. For speculation on this score, see Neustadt, *Presidential Power and the Modern Presidents,* 213.

33. On this, see, for example, Parker, *Vietnam: Strategy for a Stalemate,* 235. See also, Richard Nixon, "Don't let Salvador Become Another Vietnam," *Wall Street Journal,* 17 May 1983, 22, where Nixon says that after 1973 the United States cut promised aid to South Vietnam by over 75 percent, while the Soviet Union doubled its aid to North Vietnam.

34. That is, as a "better of worse outcomes" than national (moral and psychological) mobilization.

35. Other factors were a growing deficit owing to competition for resources by Johnson's "Great Society" programs, the pressures for future resources generated by a much accelerated Soviet counterforce missile program, and the pressures generated by the rapid growth of Japanese and West German economic growth. On this last point, see Thornton, *Nixon-Kissinger Years,* 8–9.

36. "The principles of a democracy are freedom and equality and these principles . . . exist in a state of perpetual tension with the idea of statesmanship. . . .

The democratic statesman must make the most and best of the democracy by appealing to principles which threaten to tear the democracy apart." Morton Frisch and Richard Stevens, eds., *American Political Thought: The Philosophic Dimension of American Statesmanship* (New York: Charles Scribner's Sons, 1971), 8.

37. Richard Nixon, *Leaders*, 343.

38. For a lengthy account, see Peter Braestrup, *Big Story: How the American Press and Television Reported the Crisis of Tet 1968 in Vietnam and Washington* (Garden City, N.Y.: Anchor Books, 1978).

39. On this see Harry G. Summers, Jr., *On Strategy: A Critical Analysis of the Vietnam War* (Novato, Calif.: Presidio Press, 1982), 133–34. See also the video documentary, "Television's Vietnam," produced by Accuracy in Media, Inc., Washington, D.C., 1984, 1985.

40. For the undocumented assertion that Nixon was initially "set up" for "obstruction of justice charges" (which led to his resignation) by the eastern wing of the Republican party, led from within the administration by former Attorney General John Mitchell, see Thornton, *Nixon-Kissinger Years*, 154. On the role of the "establishment media," see Johnson, *Modern Times*, 648–53.

41. For this characterization, see Cleva, *Henry Kissinger and the American Approach*, 203.

42. Nixon, *Leaders*, 342–43. Although Nixon wrote these lines after leaving office, there is no reason to assume he had not discerned such general effects long before he got to the presidency.

43. Recall, in this context, Huey Long's remarks, cited in the introduction to this book: "A perfect democracy can come close to looking like a dictatorship, a democracy in which people are so satisfied they have no complaint."

44. For this formulation, see Joseph Cropsey, "The United States as Regime," in *The Moral Foundations of the American Republic*, ed. Robert Horwitz, 3d ed. (Charlottesville: University Press of Virginia, 1986), 180.

45. Cleva, *Henry Kissinger and the American Approach*, 203.

Chapter 8. The Modern Challenges to Statesmanship

1. For development of this theme, see Leslie Goodrich Rubin, *The Republic of Aristotle: Politics and the Best Political Regime*, Ph.D. dissertation, Boston College, 1985 (Ann Arbor, Michigan: University Microfilms International, 1986).

2. For development of this idea, see Wendell J. Coats, Jr., *The Activity of Politics and Related Essays* (London and Toronto: Associated University Presses, 1989).

3. For development of this theme, see Wendell J. Coats, Jr., *A Theory of Republican Character and Related Essays* (London and Toronto: Associated University Presses, 1994).

4. For an analysis of Tocqueville's predictions about these tendencies, see Peter Augustine Lawler, "Democracy and Pantheism," in *Interpreting Tocqueville's Democracy in America*, ed. Ken Masugi (Savage, Md.: Rowman and Littlefield Publishers, Inc., 1991), 96–120. See also Eric Voegelin, *The New Science of Politics* (Chicago: University of Chicago Press, 1952), 143 and 173–78.

5. For a balanced account of the southern view of the constitutional issues involved, see Marshall L. DeRosa, *The Confederate Constitution of 1861: An Inquiry into American Constitutionalism* (Columbia: University of Missouri Press, 1991).

6. See chap. 3, 57.

7. I emphasize "explicit understanding" because in tranquil times the Ameri-

can practice of politics is quite moderate; the dangers come in times of crisis when explicit understandings become essential to the future preservation of inherited practices.

8. See chap. 7, 117.

9. Carl Schmitt, *The Concept of the Political,* trans. George Schwab, (Reprint; New Brunswick, N.J.: Rutgers University Press, 1976), 34, n. 14.

10. It is surely possible to state something so obvious without buying into the overstated (hence, inaccurate) theories of Carl Schmitt about the centrality of the friend-enemy distinction and war in the idea of the political. Schmitt's fundamental misconception, in my view, is to equate "the political" with what is more accurately seen as undifferentiated and subpolitical instances of very intense competition between various human groups. (More generally Schmitt makes the philosophic error of continually taking his bearings from the worst case—*Ernstfall,* thus mistaking a precondition for a part of the whole and attempting to explain the "higher" in terms of the "lower.") As I use it, "the political" refers to a civilized achievement, a complex of characteristics for dealing with such intense, subpolitical antagonisms. Hence its ultimate reliance on the threat of armed force makes it "more intense" than labor arbitration, for example, but it may not be defined primarily in terms of its intensity. "Politics" refers (if it is not to make a superfluous distinction) to a complex of civilized practices for moderating immoderations without the misguided, utopian intent to see all the immoderations permanently removed. On this subject, see also my review essay of Christian Meier's *The Greek Discovery of Politics* ("Aristotelian Doubts About Meier on the Political") in *Polis* 11, 2 (1992), 178–83.

11. See, for a discussion, Jürgen Habermas, *Moral Consciousness and Communicative Action,* trans. Christian Lenhardt and Shierry Weber Nicholson (Cambridge, Mass.: MIT Press, 1990), 196–211. In my view there is laced throughout this neo-Marxist perspective a latent threat of coercion; see, for example, 58: "Only an intersubjective process of reaching understanding can produce an agreement that is reflexive in nature; only it can give the participants the knowledge that they have collectively become convinced of something." See also on this general point, Jürgen Habermas, *Autonomy and Solidarity: Interviews,* ed. Peter Drews (Thetford, Norfolk, England: The Thetford Press, 1986), 185.

12. I do not mean to imply that the "old" politics can not accommodate the idea of universal truths but merely that discourse about such truths must take the form of persuasive utterance urging prudent courses of action in order to enter the realm of political speech. See Michael Oakeshott, *On Human Conduct* (Oxford: Oxford University Press, 1975), 177.

13. "Politics" is used in its careful sense and is distinguished from military, technocratic, corporatist, theocratic, and other less free forms of "social integration."

14. On democracy's hostility to even demonstrably necessary political abstractions, see the title essay to Wendell J. Coats, Jr., *A Theory of Republican Character,* 15–62.

Bibliography

BOOKS

Allen, W. B., ed. *George Washington: A Collection*. Indianapolis: Liberty Classics, 1988.

Ambrose, Stephen E. *Nixon: Ruin and Recovery*. New York: Simon and Schuster, 1991.

Aristotle. *Nicomachean Ethics*. Translated by H. Rackham. Cambridge, Mass.: Loeb Classical Library/Harvard University Press, 1934.

Aron, Raymond. *The Imperial Republic: The United States and the World, 1945–1973*. Translated by Frank Jellinik. Cambridge, Mass.: Winthrop Publishers, 1974.

Barker, Ernest, ed. *The Politics of Aristotle*. London: Oxford University Press, 1958.

Barzun, Jacques. *Lincoln the Literary Genius*. Evanston, Ill., Evanston Publishing Co., 1960.

Bauer, P. T. *Dissent on Development*. Revised edition. Cambridge, Mass.: Harvard University Press, 1976.

Charnwood, Lord. *Abraham Lincoln*. 2d ed. New York: Henry Hold & Co., 1917.

Churchill, Winston. *The Second World War (The Gathering Storm)*. Boston: Houghton-Mifflin Co., 1985.

Cicero. *De Officiis*. Translated by Walter Miller. Cambridge, Mass.: Harvard University Press/Loeb Classical Library, 1913.

Clements, Kendrick A. *The Presidency of Woodrow Wilson*. Lawrence: University Press of Kansas, 1992.

Cleva, Gregory A. *Henry Kissinger and the American Approach to Foreign Policy*. London and Toronto: Associated University Press, 1989.

Coats, Wendell J., Jr. *The Activity of Politics and Related Essays*. London and Toronto: Associated University Press, 1989.

———. *A Theory of Republican Character and Related Essays*. London and Toronto: Associated University Press, 1994.

Cooper, James Fenimore. *The American Democrat*. New York: Alfred & Knopf, 1931.

Cronon, E. David, ed. *The Political Thought of Woodrow Wilson*. Indianapolis: The Robbs-Merrill Company, Inc., 1965.

Deane, Herbert A. *The Political and Social Ideas of St. Augustine*. New York: Columbia University Press, 1963.

DeRosa, Marshall L. *The Confederate Constitution of 1861: An Inquiry into American Constitutionalism*. Columbia: University of Missouri Press, 1991.

Dewey, John, ed. *The Living Thoughts of Thomas Jefferson.* New York: Longman, Green and Co., 1940.

Dickson, Peter W. *Kissinger and the Meaning of History.* Cambridge: Cambridge University Press, 1978.

Eidelberg, Paul A. *A Discourse on Statesmanship: The Design and Transformation of the American Polity.* Urbana: University of Illinois Press, 1974.

Emery, Noemie. *Alexander Hamilton: An Intimate Portrait.* New York: G. P. Putnam's Sons, 1982.

————. *Washington: A Biography.* New York: G. P. Putnam's Sons, 1976.

Fitzpatrick, John C., ed. *The Writings of George Washington,* vol. 36. Washington, D.C., U.S.G.P.O., 1941.

Flaumenhaft, Harvey. *The Effective Republic: Administration and Constitution in the Thought of Alexander Hamilton.* Durham, N.C.: Duke University Press, 1992.

Foster, Michael B. *The Political Philosophies of Plato and Hegel.* Oxford: Claredon Press, 1935.

Friedman, Lawrence. *The Evolution of Nuclear Strategy.* New York: St. Martin's Press, 1983.

Frisch, Morton J., and Richard G. Stevens. *American Political Thought: The Philosophic Dimension of American Statesmanship.* New York: Charles Scribner's Sons, 1977.

Gaulle, Charles de. *War Memoirs: The Call to Honor, 1940–1942, Documents.* New York: The Viking Press, 1955.

————. *The War Memoirs of Charles de Gaulle: Unity, 1942–1944, Documents.* New York: Simon and Schuster, 1959.

————. *The Edge of the Sword.* Translated by Gerald Hopkins. New York: Criterium Books, 1960.

————. *Memoirs of Hope: Renewal and Endeavors.* New York: Simon and Schuster, 1971.

Gerth, H. H., and C. Wright Mills, eds. *From Max Weber.* New York: Oxford University Press, 1958.

Gilbert, Martin. *Churchill's Political Philosophy.* New York: Oxford University Press, 1984.

————. *Churchill: A Life.* New York: Henry Holt and Co., 1991.

Grant, Michael, ed. *Cicero on the Good Life.* London: Penguin Books, 1971.

Hamilton, Edith, and Huntington Cairns. *The Collected Dialogues of Plato.* Princeton: Princeton University Press, 1963.

Heckscher, August, ed. *The Politics of Woodrow Wilson.* New York: Harper and Brothers, 1956.

Hollifield, James and George Ross, eds. *Searching for the New France.* New York: Routledge: 1991.

Horwitz, Robert H., ed. *The Moral Foundations of the American Republic.* Charlottesville: University Press of Virginia, 1986.

Huntington, Samuel P. *The Soldier and the State.* Cambridge: Harvard University Press, 1957.

Isaacson, Walter. *Kissinger: A Biography.* New York: Simon and Schuster, 1992.

Jaffa, Harry V. *Crisis of the House Divided: An Interpretation of the Issues in the Lincoln-Douglas Debates.* Chicago: University of Chicago Press, 1982.

Jaffa, Harry, ed. *Statesmanship: Essays in Honor of Sir Winston Churchill.* Durham, N.C.: Carolina Academic Press, 1981.

Johnson, Paul. *Modern Times: The World from the Twenties to the Eighties.* New York: Harper & Row, 1983.

———. *Modern Times: The World from the Twenties to the Nineties.* Revised edition. New York: Harper Collins Publishers, 1991.

Jung, C. G. *Psychology and Religion.* New Haven: Yale University Press, 1938.

Kimball, Warren F. *The Juggler: Franklin Roosevelt as Wartime Statesman.* Princeton: Princeton University Press, 1991.

Kissinger, Henry. *Nuclear Weapons and Foreign Policy.* New York: Harper and Brothers, 1957.

———. *White House Years.* Boston: Little, Brown and Company, 1979.

———. *Years of Upheaval.* Boston: Little, Brown and Company, 1982.

———. *Diplomacy.* New York: Simon and Schuster, 1994.

Lacouture, Jean. *de Gaulle: The Rebel 1890–1944.* Translated by Patrick O'Brian. New York: W. W. Norton and Co., 1990.

———. *de Gaulle: The Ruler, 1945–1970.* Translated by Alan Sheridan. New York: W. W. Norton & Co., 1992.

Link, Arthur S., ed. *The Papers of Woodrow Wilson,* vol. 5. Princeton: Princeton University Press, 1968.

Lodge, Henry Cabot. *George Washington.* Boston: Houghton, Mifflin and Co., 1890.

Machiavelli, Niccolo. *The Prince and the Discourses.* Edited by Max Lerner. New York: The Modern Library, 1950.

———. *The Prince.* Translated by George Bull. New York: Penguin Books, 1961.

Malraux, André. *Felled Oaks: Conversations with de Gaulle.* New York: Holt, Rinehart and Winston, 1972.

Masugi, Ken, ed. *Interpreting Tocqueville's Democracy in America,* Savage, Md.: Rowman and Littlefield Publications, Inc., 1991.

Matthews, Christopher. *Hardball: How Politics Is Played Told by One Who Knows the Game.* New York: Harper and Row, 1988.

McDonald, Forrest. *The Presidency of George Washington.* Lawrence: University Press of Kansas, 1974.

McPherson, James M. *Abraham Lincoln and the Second American Revolution.* New York: Oxford University Press, 1991.

Merleau-Ponty, Maurice, *Humanism and Terror.* Translated by John O'Neill. Boston: Beacon Press, 1969.

Monnet, Jean. *Memoirs.* Translated by Richard Wayne. Garden City, N.Y.: Doubleday, 1978.

Morrisey, Will. *Reflections on De Gaulle: Political Founding in Modernity.* Lanham, Md.; University Press of America, 1983.

Neustadt, Richard E. *Presidential Power and the Modern Presidents.* New York: The Free Press, 1990.

Nichols, Mary P. *Citizens and Statesmen: A Study of Aristotle's Politics.* Savage, Md.: Rowman & Littlefield Publishers, Inc., 1992.

Nixon, Richard. *The Memoirs of Richard Nixon.* New York: Grosset and Dunlap, 1978.

————. *Leaders*. New York: Warner Books, Inc., 1982.

————. *In the Arena: A Memoir of Victory, Defeat and Renewal*. New York: Simon and Schuster, 1990.

Oakeshott, Michael J. *On Human Conduct*. Oxford: Clarendon Press, 1975.

Paret, Peter, ed. *Maker of Modern Strategy*. Princeton: Princeton University Press, 1986.

Parker, F. Charles, IV. *Vietnam: Strategy for a Stalemate*. New York: Paragon House, 1989.

Ruggiero, Guido de. *The History of European Liberalism*. Translated by R. G. Collingwood. Oxford: Oxford University Press, 1927.

St. Augustine. *The City of God Against the Pagans*. Volume 6, Trans. William G. Greene, Cambridge, MA: Loeb Classical Library/Harvard University Press, 1969.

Schall, James V. *Reason, Revelation and the Foundations of Political Philosophy*. Baton Rouge: Louisiana State University Press, 1987.

Schelling, Thomas. *Arms and Influence*. New Haven: Yale University Press, 1966.

Schmitt, Carl. *The Concept of the Political*. Translated by George Schwab. New Brunswick, N.J.: Rugers University Press, 1976.

Shaw, Archer H., ed. *The Lincoln Encyclopedia*. New York: The MacMillan Company, 1950.

Shonfield, Andrew. *Modern Capitalism: The Changing Balance of Public and Private Power*. London: Oxford University Press, 1969.

Skinner, B. F. *Beyond Freedom and Dignity*. New York: Bantam-Vintage Books, 1972.

Stourzh, Gerald. *Alexander Hamilton and the Idea of Republican Government*. Stanford: Stanford University Press, 1970.

Summers, Harry G. *On Strategy: A Critical Analysis of the Vietnam War*. Novato, Calif.: Presidio Press, 1982.

Syrett, Harold C., ed. *The Papers of Alexander Hamilton*, vol. 25. New York: Columbia University Press, 1977.

Thornton, Richard. *The Nixon Kissinger Years: Reshaping America's Foreign Policy*. New York: Paragon Books, 1989.

Tocqueville, Alexis de. *Democracy in America*. New York: Vintage Books, 1945.

Tucker, Robert C., ed. *The Lenin Anthology*. New York: W. W. Norton and Co., 1975.

Tucker, Robert W. *Nation or Empire? The Debate Over American Foreign Policy*. Baltimore, Md.: The John Hopkins Press, 1988.

Tuveson, Ernest Lee. *Redeemer Nation: The Idea of America's Millennial Role*. Chicago: The University of Chicago Press, 1968.

Voegelin, Eric. *The New Science of Politics*. Chicago: University of Chicago Press, 1952.

Wallop, Malcolm, and Angelo Codevilla. *The Arms Control Delusion*. San Francisco: ICS Press, 1987.

Williams, T. Harry. *Huey Long*. New York: Vintage Books, 1981.

Yanarella, Ernest J. *The Missile Defense Controversy.* Lexington: University of Kentucky Press, 1977.

ARTICLES

Adair, Douglass, and Marvin Harvey. "Was Alexander Hamilton a Christian Statesman?" *William and Mary Quarterly* 12 (April 1985): 308–29.

Bacevich, A. J. "Gays and the Military Culture." *National Review* 45 no. 8 (26 April 1993): 26–31.

Bishirijian, Richard J. "Croly, Wilson, and the American Civil Religion." *Modern Age,* 23 (Winter 1979) 33–38.

Bradford, M. E. "From the Family of the Lion." *Chronicles* (December 1991): 31–32.

Coats, Wendell J., Jr. "The Ideology of Arms Control." *Journal of Contemporary Studies* 5:3 (Summer 1982): 3–15.

———. "The Malingering McNamara Model for the Use of U.S. Military Force." *Strategic Review* 17 no. 4 (Fall 1989): 18–30.

Ellis, Richard, and Aaron Wildavsky. "'Greatness' Re-visited: Evaluating the Performance of Early American Presidents in Terms of Cultural Dilemmas." *Presidential Studies Quarterly* 21 no. 1 (Winter 1991): 15–34.

Holmes, Stephen Taylor. "Aristippus in and out of Athens." *American Political Science Review* 73 no. 1 (March 1979), 113–33.

Joffe, Josef. "In Defense of Henry Kissinger." *Commentary* 96 no. 6 (December 1992): 49–52.

Johnson, Paul. "In Praise of Richard Nixon." *Commentary* 86 no. 4 (October 1988): 50–53.

Kissinger, Henry. "NATO: The Next Thirty Years by Henry Kissinger." *Survival* 21 no. 6 (November–December 1979): 264–68.

———. "The White Revolutionary: Reflections on Bismark." *Daedalus* 97 (Summer 1988): 888–921.

Loss, Richard. "The Political Thought of President George Washington." *Presidential Studies Quarterly* 19 no. 3 (Summer 1989): 471–90.

Phelps, Glenn A. "George Washington and the Paradox of Party." *Presidential Studies Quarterly* 19 no. 4 (Summer 1989): 733–45.

Reynolds, David. "Rethinking Anglo-American Relations." *International Affairs* 65 no. 1 (Winter 1988/89): 89–111.

Walling, Karl. "America's Machiavellian Moment Reconsidered: War, Liberty and Virtue in the Commercial Republicanism of Alexander Hamilton" (paper presented at American Political Science Association annual meeting, Washington, D.C., 1993).

Index

149